"A lively and comprehensive set of readings that cover all the key elements of state politics. The topics are carefully selected and the essays engaging—highly recommended."

Kevin B. Smith
University of Nebraska—Lincoln

"This book is an uncommonly witty and lively examination of state and local government. These enjoyable case studies will engage every reader."

John C. LePete
Palo Alto College

"This timely volume provides a focused analysis on the most pressing issues facing state and local governments, applying the latest in political science and public policy research to ongoing social problems. The applied nature of the content as well as the end of chapter discussion questions make this a valuable resource for students and faculty."

Christopher W. Larimer
University of Northern Iowa

STATE AND LOCAL POLITICS

This book is the first of its kind to take concepts directly from the most commonly used textbooks in state and local politics and apply them directly to current events. It presents twelve chapters of case studies, richly detailing key topics ranging from how the comparative method can be used to understand the similarities and differences between diverse places, to a look at how state governments have taken the lead on COVID-19, environmental policy, civil rights, gun control, college tuition regulation, cybersecurity and elections, sex offenders, and many more subjects of contemporary interest. It devotes a complete chapter to local-level politics in Nevada, Florida, and Iowa, and wraps up with a unique chapter on regional governance bridging between states and localities. This detailed and highly readable book is designed to complement traditional state and local textbooks. It is also of interest to students of public administration, public policy, urban politics, and intro to American politics.

Jayme L. Renfro is an Associate Professor of Political Science at the University of Northern Iowa. She enjoys teaching public policy and administration to both undergraduate and graduate students and has earned university- and college wide teaching awards. She is co-author, with Kevin B. Smith, of *State and Local Government 2013–2014*. She enjoys books, her husband, travelling, playing darts, her children, cake, and naps (not in that order).

STATE AND LOCAL POLITICS

Cases and Topics

Jayme L. Renfro

R Routledge
Taylor & Francis Group

NEW YORK AND LONDON

First published 2021
by Routledge
52 Vanderbilt Avenue, New York, NY 10017

and by Routledge
2 Park Square, Milton Park, Abingdon, Oxon, OX14 4RN

Routledge is an imprint of the Taylor & Francis Group, an informa business

Library of Congress Cataloging-in-Publication Data
Names: Renfro, Jayme L., author.
Title: State and local politics: cases and topics/Jayme L. Renfro.
Description: New York, NY: Routledge, 2021. | Includes bibliographical
    references and index.
Identifiers: LCCN 2020049382 (print) | LCCN 2020049383 (ebook) |
    ISBN 9780367174491 (hardback) | ISBN 9780367174552 (paperback) |
    ISBN 9780429056895 (ebook)
Subjects: LCSH: State governments–United States–Case studies. | Local
    government–United States–Case studies. | Central-local government
    relations–United States–Case studies. | United States–Politics and
    government.
Classification: LCC JK2408 .R52 2021 (print) | LCC JK2408 (ebook) |
    DDC 320.473–dc23
LC record available at https://lccn.loc.gov/2020049382
LC ebook record available at https://lccn.loc.gov/2020049383

ISBN: 9780367174491 (hbk)
ISBN: 9780367174552 (pbk)
ISBN: 9780429056895 (ebk)

Typeset in Bembo
by KnowledgeWorks Global Ltd.

This book was conceived at the same time as my son. Both he and it have kept me up at night. This one is for you and your sister, buddy

CONTENTS

Introduction   1

1 The Comparative Method   3
  Borders and BBQ: KCK and KCMO and the Dividing
     Lines of Government and Culture 4
  Georgia on My Mind 6
  Using the Laboratories of Democracy to Keep People Healthy 11
  Note 13
  Works Cited 13

2 Federalism and Intergovernmental Relations   15
  Hurricanes, Floods, and Tornados Oh My! The High
     Cost of Disaster Recovery 16
  Federal Ownership of Land, or, When Nevada isn't
     Actually Nevada 19
  FedEd: Investigating Civil Rights Violations in Schools 22
  Note 25
  Works Cited 26

3 State Constitutions   27
  The Right to Hunt and Fish and Hang Out on the
     Front Porch 28
  Problems in Euclid and the Limitations of the
     Ohio Constitution 31
  From Plastic Bags to Guns: Preemption Laws
     and an Evolving Political Landscape 34
  Works Cited 37

4 Budgeting, Finance, and Fiscal Policy   38
  Tax Cuts and College Tuition, A Louisiana Story 38
  Is Grandpa Bankrupting Your City? A Look at Debts
    and Liabilities 42
  Isn't That Their Job? How State Legislatures End Up Not
    Passing Budgets 45
  Works Cited 49

5 Elections and Political Participation   51
  Social Pressure and Voter Turnout 51
  Cybersecurity and Election Systems: When Is It Time
    to Panic? 54
  Is the Internet a Tool or a Distraction for Increasing
    Political Participation? 57
  Notes 60
  Works Cited 60

6 Political Parties and Interest Groups   61
  A Two-Party System Requires Two Parties: Democrats
    in the South 62
  (Maybe Don't) Show Me the Money: Big Money's Influence
    in State and Local Elections 65
  ALEC and the Use and Misuse of Model Bills 69
  Works Cited 73

7 State Legislatures   75
  Descriptive Representation and Policy Outcomes:
    Do Female Legislators Matter? 75
  Professional Versus Citizen Legislatures 78
  Jeffrey Epstein and the Varying Interpretation of Federal Sex
    Offender Registry Laws 81
  Works Cited 83

8 State Executive Leadership   85
  When It All Goes Wrong: The Impeachments
    of Governor Robert Bently and Eric Greitens 86
  The Gubernatorial Incumbency Advantage 89
  Can a State Make a Difference on Environmental
    Policy? California Is Giving It a Shot 92
  Note 95
  Works Cited 96

9 State Court Systems   97
   In Loco Parentis 97
   Judicial Recall: How the Brock Turner Case Turned California
      on Its Head 101
   Selling Beer to Alcoholics: The Nebraska State Supreme
      Court and the Whiteclay Problem 103
   Note 106
   Works Cited 106

10 The Bureaucracy   108
   Interesting Work, Good Benefits, and Job Security:
      Why Work for the Government? 108
   Bureaucrat Bashing in the Era of Civil Service Shame 112
   Verruckt and the Case for Increased Government Regulation
      of Amusement Parks 115
   Notes 118
   Works Cited 118

11 Local Governments   120
   Handling an "Alien" Invasion in a Small Desert Town 120
   Council-Manager or Strong Mayor? Clearwater,
      FL Decides 123
   Postville, IA: A Town Recovers from a Major
      Immigration Raid 126
   Note 129
   Works Cited 129

12 Regional Governance   130
   The Sprawliest Sprawl—Not Los Angeles? 130
   The Houston Metro Area: Flood City U.S.A. 133
   Tiebout Gets Schooled: The Indirect Benefits of Public
      Schools on Community Satisfaction 135
   Works Cited 139

Conclusion   *140*
Index   *142*

INTRODUCTION

During the summer of 2017, President Trump announced that the United States would officially be pulling out of the Paris Climate Accord—an agreement nearly every country in the world (save for two, Syria and Ecuador) signed agreeing to work to reduce greenhouse gasses. In response to this news, several states such as California, New York, Hawaii, Massachusetts, and Virginia, as well as mayors from cities from Los Angeles to New York, Houston to Seattle signed on to continue the effort to fulfill America's pledge on the agreement. Even smaller towns like Fayetteville, Arkansas, and Ambler, Pennsylvania have joined the movement.

One may wonder what kind of impact states and localities could even have on something like the environment when the federal government isn't on board, but that perspective underplays the real power of state and local governments. In a letter to the Secretary General of the United Nations, New York Mayor Michael Bloomberg was confident that sub-national actors would be able to uphold the accord without the cooperation of the federal government. He wrote, "While the executive branch of the U.S. government speaks on behalf of our nation in matters of foreign affairs, it does not determine many aspects of whether and how the United States takes action on climate change." (Tabuchi and Fountain 2017)

Bloomberg's position that the majority of the decisions that influence the U.S.'s part in global climate change are made by non-national entities like cities and states is more broadly applicable as well. State and local governments are intimately involved in our day-to-day lives, even if we don't realize it most of the time. Trash collectors start their duties at dawn (or before in some cases!), busses start shuttling people to work and school, you brush your teeth using the water that is likely a public utility. The roads that we drive on and the sidewalks that we walk on are built and maintained by state and local employees. You might be reading this as you attend a school that is either funded or regulated (or both) by state and local governments. Do you eat at restaurants? If you tend not to get food poisoning, you might want to thank a local health inspector. Thinking of starting a business? You are going to need to talk to some state and local officials. Same thing if you want to get married. Most of the decisions that have a practical influence on our lives are made at the state and local levels.

Is this all sounding a little intimidating or intrusive? It is true, government is everywhere, however it is important to understand that each of these intrusions were brought about because someone asked for them. We are currently living in an era where governments are trying to reduce the number of services that they provide; generally, government officials are not seeking out new ways to get involved in your day-to-day activities—remember, government officials are citizens as well who are subject to most of these "intrusions" as well. Rather, groups of citizens or businesses see a need, an area in which they believe lives could be improved, or people or interests protected. Even as the majority of Americans support lower taxes, they continue to insist on things like crime control, road safety, and elementary schools.

State and local governments control or have a strong hand in virtually all domestic government policy in the U.S., yet people tend to pay far more attention to politics on the national stage—and that is if they are even paying attention at all. And this is why you, as a student of a class that has assigned this book, have a particular responsibility to learn about state and local politics. Your textbook will introduce you to the topics and concepts that are crucial to know if you are to master this subject, and this book of case studies will give you an opportunity to see how those concepts apply in real-life situations—and even to apply them yourselves. The better you are able to do this, the better you will be able to interact with, and maybe even influence, the very policies that affect you the most through your life.

1

THE COMPARATIVE METHOD

Ok, now you understand the importance of knowing about state and local governments and their policies. That's great, right? Sure, but it isn't enough. In order to actually learn about state and local governments, one needs to develop a systematic approach to looking at the similarities and differences—also known as variance—between comparable units.

The comparative method is a fundamental tool of analysis. It greatly improves our power of description, and plays a role in idea formation by illuminating potentially interesting and meaningful similarities and differences among cases. Comparison is often used in hypothesis testing, and it can contribute to the discovery of new hypotheses as well.

The forms of comparison used in the study of state and local politics vary widely, however most boil down to the systematic analysis of a small number of cases—either two or more different places compared to one another, or one place compared to itself over time. In this chapter, you will read case studies that are examples of both. First, you will read about Kansas City, a city that spills over the border into two different states. This unique situation sheds light on some pretty profound differences between the two states that share it. Next, we will walk through some of the history of Georgia, from its beginnings as a small settlement to the bustling state it is now. Changes in the economy and politics since its inception allow us to compare Georgia to itself over time, developing a deeper understanding of why things are changing there so quickly today. Finally, we examine a topic that is timely and important—the COVID-19 pandemic. More specifically, we talk about the variation in how states responded to the pandemic and how that information can be used moving forward to make decisions. Taken together, these three case studies illustrate the comparative method and its potential uses for the study of state and local government.

Borders and BBQ: KCK and KCMO and the Dividing Lines of Government and Culture

In 1718, acting on a tip from a French ne'er do well, Gillaume de L'Isle mapped out an area smack in the middle of nowhere and named it after the local tribe, the Cansez. Natives and a small group of settlers coexisted peacefully in the area until a century later when Lewis and Clark appeared from the river and promptly kicked everyone out in order to start work on a new fort and village. One thing that they did keep (pretty much) was the name, though they changed it slightly from the French spelling to Kansa and later, Kansas (Kansas State Historical Society n.d.).

The town of Kansas had been around for a century if you count from when it was named, but it wasn't until 1821 that Missouri became a state. The lines were drawn between Missouri and the unincorporated lands to the west—lines that went right through the town of Kansas. So, Kansas City never really crossed the border, the border was drawn right smack through Kansas City.

No one truly considered this an issue though. Because the west side wasn't really part of anything for the next six decades, there were few complications as to where the borders were drawn. However, as the United States moved west as part of the whole Manifest Destiny thing, the area that would become the state of Kansas was settled and organized by a different group of people than those that had founded Missouri. Hence, Missouri and Kansas are different states, with a different history, culture, and population. They share a border, and, in many ways, the "town" that is now the sprawling, bustling metropolis called Kansas City[1].

When Daniel Elazar developed his political culture typology, he identified Missouri as an individualistic state and Kansas as a moralistic one. Individualistic populations see government as existing for the purpose of addressing individual goals and issues. Much like a marketplace, government should provide the goods and services that people want, prioritizing individual interests over the needs of groups/communities. A society that sees things in this way would favor such policies as cutting taxes to low rates to try to encourage individual economic benefit.

Moralistic states on the other hand, believe that government is essentially good and should be in the business of bettering society and promoting its general welfare. Group interests should be held as the ultimate focus over individual interests. Politicians are held to high standards, voting and other forms of civic participation are not only encouraged, but expected of citizens. Moralistic societies have high levels of volunteerism and voter turnout.

Many of the differences between Kansas City, Kansas and Kansas City, Missouri make perfect sense when examined thought Elazar's lens. Generally,

Kansas has higher taxes than Missouri does. The sales, income, and property taxes are all higher in KCK than they are in KCMO. On a trip down to Missouri to visit a school, the author was once told that Missouri is a "low tax, low service" state, and many believe this to be true. One resident of a KCK suburb reports that she can tell when she crosses over the border into Missouri by the way the streets are maintained. Lower taxes mean that the state has less money to put into the construction and maintenance of roads. She noted that this is especially evident during the winter when snow removal tends to be more prompt and frequent on the Kansas side of the line than on the Missouri side.

So, historically, Kansas had been the higher tax, higher service state, however in 2012, Governor Sam Brownback instituted a series of tax cuts, the likes of which most places had never seen. Income, business, and corporate taxes were lowered drastically, ostensibly to create growth—trickle-down style. Instead of the shot of adrenaline that this was supposed to be though, the Kansas economy tanked (Prokop 2014). Their credit rating dropped and their economic growth slowed to almost nothing. In order to try to balance some of the cuts and increase the money in the coffers, lawmakers increased the sales and excise taxes, however that wasn't enough. Funding for Kansas schools dropped so low that the United States Supreme Court found it to be unconstitutional. Even though things started to look up in 2019, there was a $351 million shortfall leftover from 2018 (Cohn 2019) and the pandemic of 2020 is expected to trigger further shortfalls.

It gets particularly complicated in Kansas City. Missouri and Kansas both want businesses located on their side of the border. Businesses (even if they aren't being taxed directly) are worth money to the state government. They bring jobs and economic growth to the state in addition to things like sales taxes. Thus, KCK and KCMO offer tax breaks and other economic incentives to encourage businesses to set up shop on one side or the other. The Hall Family Foundation estimated that they gave up approximately $217 million dollars in taxes from 2009-2014 in order to attract these businesses. During that time period Missouri "stole" 2,824 jobs from Kansas and Kansas "stole" 3,289 from Missouri. It appears that Kansas is winning this race, however, if you took the difference between the bounties and divide it by Kansas' half of the $217 million, each of those jobs cost Kansas about $233,333 (Hall Family Foundation 2019). One might wonder if it was worth it.

Discussion Questions

1. Do you think that Kansas might no longer be a moralistic state? Did Elazar have anything to say about the possibility of a state changing their political culture? Are there precedents in other states?

2. States have been referred to as laboratories of democracy in terms of creating policy. What can other states learn from Kansas' experiment in extreme tax cutting? What can the Federal government learn? Is the experience of a state even relevant to the Federal government?
3. How can funding for schools be a constitutional issue? Why can't a state decide that it doesn't want to fund schools at a higher level if it wants to?
4. What information about the sociodemographics of KCK and KCMO would be valuable in understanding the differences in culture between the two? Why? How might one go about obtaining this information?

Key Concepts

- Comparative method
- Variance
- Political culture
- Laboratories of democracy

For More Information:

https://kchistory.org/faq/why-there-kansas-city-both-kansas-and-missouri
https://www.bestplaces.net/compare-cities/kansas_city_mo/kansas_city_ks/people
https://www.youtube.com/watch?v=B_x_67fXtqM

Georgia on My Mind

The state of Georgia has had seven official state flags over the course of its history (New Georgia Encyclopedia 2018b). From a simple coat of arms on a blue background, through versions that included the confederate battle flag, to the current flag that is reminiscent of both the American flag and the national flag of the confederacy, these changes can easily be seen as a metaphor for a state that has undergone myriad changes itself.

Prior to the British settling in the area in the early 1700s, the land that we now know as Georgia was inhabited by the Cherokee and Creek nations. Like many of the American colonies, Georgia was founded as a refuge for those suffering religious persecution at home and as a place for hard-working, unemployed, or even debt prisoner Englishmen to go and work for the crown while creating new lives for themselves. Trustees were tasked with choosing the new settlers from a long list of applicants, largely choosing tradesman and those who intended to open small businesses (and interestingly but perhaps unsurprisingly no debt prisoners) (Georgia Historical Society n.d.).

Over the years, a discontent with British rule over the colonies spread through the new lands, however Georgia was generally less unhappy than most.

Georgians had set up a relatively satisfactory, and mutually beneficial, system with England, shipping raw materials over and receiving manufactured goods in return. Eventually though, however well this back and forth was working, the British managed to overstep and irritate the wrong Georgians with some uneven trade deals and high taxes. Georgians, it turned out, did not much care for big government taking advantage of business owners and farmers. This sentiment led to the creation of an independent colonial government, and has continued to shape the culture of Georgia to this day.

Georgia continued to chug along as an agricultural center, and if you will remember back to middle school history class, in 1793, Eli Whitney invented the cotton gin. This was a particularly big development in Georgia, and the ability to separate cotton seed from lint of the plant with a machine allowed for the development of bigger and more productive farms devoted to growing and processing cotton (Georgia Humanities 2009). Slavery wasn't new to Georgia, however these larger plantations made slavery more profitable than before, as farmers could now clean the cotton as quickly as they had hands to pick it. By 1860, Georgia had both the highest number of slaves and slaveholders in the Deep South and of all the colonies only Virginia had more (New Georgia Encyclopedia 2017).

Georgian culture and the ensuing politics then developed through the combination of an anti-big government sentiment and some pretty significant cotton money rolling in on the backs of slaves. Essentially, Georgia was more economically prosperous than most of the other southern states and just wanted everyone to leave them alone to keep doing what they had been doing. The election of President Lincoln in 1860 made that impossible. Where Georgia conservatives had been pretty politically moderate before, this attack on states' rights from the federal government was not to be tolerated. How dare some northerner in Washington tell them that they probably shouldn't own people! The legislature appropriated money to grow the state militia in short order, followed quickly by an official secession in January of 1861.

Participation in the Confederates' war on the Union did not change the people of Georgia's basic worldview on government though. They were still states' rights believers through and through. They did not believe in the conscription of soldiers to the Confederate army or in sending the Georgia militia to other states to fight. They were not supportive of the use of private property or railroads for military uses. They were willing to fight the Union in support of their way of life and mode of income, but they weren't ready to change themselves to achieve victory.

The war was over in 1865 and even though the Confederates surrendered, it took Georgia a while to accept the outcome and its consequences. The United States required some conditions of the states that had seceded before they were allowed to rejoin the union, and Georgian leaders weren't having it. It wasn't until three years later that the state legislature complied with the federal requirements and officially became part of the United States again. This is not to say that everything was all peaches and rainbows though. One of the conditions that was required of the former confederate states was that they allow every man to vote (not women though, that would come later). The influx of new black voters meant that black officials were elected to office for the first time. This did not sit well with some of the white men who were used to running things. After all, some of these black men had just been slaves!

Black politicians elected during the Reconstruction period were not really ever allowed to govern effectively and this led to most of them losing their offices. Black voters were also suppressed, threatened with violence for showing up or coerced into voting for white candidates. Despite the intentions of the federal government, black Georgians never became politically powerful. In fact, Reconstruction backlash and good ol' fashioned racism collided to usher in the Jim Crow era and solidify black Georgians' place as second-class citizens.

Wars are expensive to clean up, and the loss of the prosperous slavery-based economy was tough on Georgia. Sharecroppers filled the cotton-picking jobs for little or no pay until the boll weevil showed up in the early 20th century and devastated the state's cotton crops. Hundreds of thousands of the states' agricultural workers abandoned the state. It is estimated that by 1930 their numbers had dropped by almost half (New Georgia Encyclopedia 2018a). The flourishing, prosperous state was now struggling mightily. And it only got worse. Cotton prices had dropped considerably during World War I and then the Great Depression hit the country hard. President Roosevelt attempted to alleviate the suffering of the large class of extremely poor rural Americans by lowering agricultural production in order to raise crop prices, however this meant that many farmers ended up without a job. Low-wage employers, like textile mills, sprung up around the state, taking advantage of the cheap, non-union labor that was so plentiful.

World War II brought the Great Depression to an end, boosting economies all around the nation. Georgia in particular felt the benefits. Soldiers poured into Fort Benning in Columbus, which was the largest infantry training post in the world at that time. In Marietta, the Bell Aircraft Corporation employed more than 28,000 workers making B-29 Bombers. Ports at Brunswick and Savannah were bustling with shipbuilders, with one company, Southeastern Shipbuilding Corporation, employing more than 15,000 Georgians (Zainaldin 2017).

These war support activities had an enormous impact on Georgia. Between 1940 and 1950, the average income almost tripled. The state was prosperous once again.

Georgia, like the rest of the south, had been solidly under the blanket of the Democratic Party since the Reconstruction. Real political contests were not held during general elections but during the candidate selection process. We have to remember though that the Democratic party of history is not the same as the Democratic party of today. In fact, through the realignment process, the party we call Democratic today is far more akin to the Republican party of the past and vice versa. Georgia's voters have largely favored conservative policies on taxes, moral values, and security. These policies were historically associated with the Democratic Party. Further, there was a strong current of segregationist sentiment running through this part of the country that many Democratic leaders were happy to take advantage of in order to win election. It was quite common for a candidate to openly court the support of the Ku Klux Klan and similar groups in order to garner votes.

The Democratic "Solid South" monopoly first showed signs of weakness in the late 1940s when many southerners grew uneasy with the desegregationist policies proposed by President Harry Truman. Later, the signing of the Civil Rights Act of 1964 by President Lyndon Johnson led many Southern Democrats to vote for the Republican candidate, Barry Goldwater during the following election. Georgians voted for a Republican President for the first time in history. They voted for George Wallace in 1968 from the conservative American Independent Party, and have stayed pretty solidly Republican in most elections since then. There are three exceptions, however. Unsurprisingly, Georgians voted for their own native son Jimmy Carter, a Democrat, in both 1975 and 1980, and then in 1992, they went for Bill Clinton, not a Georgian but a southerner and a Democrat by a very small margin.

While the state continues to support a relatively bustling agribusiness sector (the number one fruit crop in the Peach State is the blueberry), much of the manufacturing that had sprung up in the rural areas for the cheap labor have departed for even cheaper labor in foreign lands. The agricultural industry has attracted thousands of workers, many of whom are Latino. This has led to some areas that were previously predominantly white to become more racially diverse.

Georgia has also become an attractive location for large business. There are eighteen Fortune 500 companies headquartered there, including Coca-Cola, Delta Airlines, Home Depot, and Aflac (Allison 2020). The success of these businesses has attracted a more diverse population to the cities as well. In 1980, Georgia contained around 5.5 million citizens, 72% of whom were white, 26% black, and a mere 2% other (U.S. Census Bureau 1983). Today, more than 10 million people call Georgia home, and the people are more diverse. The state currently is 60% white, 32% black, 10% Latino, and 4% Asian (U.S. Census Bureau 2019).

These demographic shifts were a large part of the prediction that Georgia was on the verge of swinging back to blue. Historically, black voters have tended to vote for Democratic candidates, and this is largely true of Latino voters as well. In 2020, for example, more than twice as many African Americans voted in Georgia than in 2016 and for the first time in decades, the state chose the Democratic candidate for president.

The extraordinary increase in turnout among black voters in Georgia is only partially explained by the increase in diversity in the state. In 2018 Stacey Abrams, a black lawyer and voting rights activist ran for governor. She lost by only 50,000 votes in a race where the winner, Brian Kemp who was the Secretary of State at the time, had purged more than 1.4 million overwhelmingly minority voters from the registration rolls prior to the election. Abrams and other voting right advocates like Nse Ufot, Helen Butler, Tamieka Atkins and Deborah Scott (notably all black women) used the momentum from the narrow race to start a massive voter registration drive. Organizers in Georgia helped register more than 800,000 new voters since the 2018 Gubernatorial race, half of whom are not white and almost half of whom are under 30. Both of those groups tend to vote for Democratic candidates.

It is predicted that Georgia will become a majority-minority state by 2025, and it is possible that this change could spark even more political changes. Considering all of the changes already seen by the state of Georgia, perhaps this wouldn't be as surprising as it first appears. On the other hand, it is possible that the people of Georgia have not changed so much, as the world has changed around them. Only time will tell.

Discussion Questions

1. What is Georgia's political culture classification, per Elazar's typology? Does it seem to be accurate, especially considering all of the changes that Georgia has undergone?
2. Considering Georgia's attitude toward big government historically, what do you think they feel toward devolution generally? What evidence is there of this?
3. How do changing demographics change the political climate in a state? Are there other states where we have seen these changes? What might we expect to see in Georgia moving forward?
4. The major political parties in the U.S. have changed positions over the years. Have the people of Georgia changed as well, or have they remained the same and we just use different labels now? What information might be useful in making this determination?

Key Concepts

- Comparative method
- Devolution
- Political culture
- Sociodemographics
- Variance

For More Information:

http://nymag.com/intelligencer/2018/11/changing-southern-democratic-party.html
https://pubs.aeaweb.org/doi/pdf/10.1257/aer.20161413
https://www.motherjones.com/kevin-drum/2015/11/why-did-democrats-lose-white-south/

Using the Laboratories of Democracy to Keep People Healthy

In 1932, Supreme Court Justice Louis Brandeis wrote the dissenting opinion in the case New State Ice Company v. Liebmann. He discussed how "a single courageous state may, if its citizens choose, serve as a laboratory; and try novel social and economic experiments without risk to the rest of the country." This concept describes how the federal system works; states have some level of autonomy to act as "laboratories" to create and test policies on a smaller scale than nationally.

In early 2020, a new strain of infectious disease called coronavirus started to spread in the United States. It was declared a pandemic by the World Health Organization on March 11, 2020. Two days later, the federal government declared a state of emergency in order to enable a bigger federal response to the pandemic, but by then many states had already taken action, including having made emergency declarations of their own. Making official statements that something is an "emergency" or a "disaster" allows the President or governors to use certain emergency powers and to access money that is set aside for cases just like this.

And so they did. Every single state took action, but the actions they took, when they took them, if and when they rolled them back ... well, this is where we have the opportunity to use the comparative method. And there are organizations collecting all of this information so that researchers and policymakers can do just that.

The Kaiser Family Foundation (now known as KFF) has been around since 1948 as a non-profit organization focusing on national health issues. They do policy analysis and research on health-related topics and provide that information free of charge to the public so that people can better understand these issues. They are a treasure trove of data and analysis on topics ranging from HIV/AIDS to racial equity in health policy to insurance coverage. And they have more recently become a gold mine for information on the COVID-19 pandemic.

Because of the variation in the way the states have handled the pandemic, it is possible to use the KFF website to understand more about the implications of different policy choices. For instance, if you were interested in the effects of the different levels of having restaurants open, you could go and look at their data on that topic (KFF 2020). Then you could see if (controlling for things like population and population density and other appropriate variables) there is a relationship between restaurants being open and, say, the positivity rate in that area. That could be awfully handy if you were a policymaker trying to make a decision about whether to reduce capacity or close restaurants when the virus reaches a certain level in your state.

During the pandemic we have seen an expansion in the use of telehealth services. It was deemed risky to venture out to the doctor's office in person, so for many types of visits we transitioned to video calls. Expanded access to telehealth services was ordered in 36 states, but even within those states there was variation. In some places, there was expanded coverage for a broad set of services and in others, it was only for limited services. Some states mandated that the insurance reimbursement rates be the same as they are for in-office visits and some did not. Some states required options for telehealth options for behavioral health and others did not. And then even within all of these, some made these changes permanent and others made them temporary (KFF 2020).

The beauty of the "laboratories of democracy" and the comparative method is that we can use this data to see what works best, and then once we do that, we have the opportunity to change paths and make better policy. If it turns out that telehealth appointments lead to bad health outcomes because doctors miss seeing things, we will catch that in the data. Or, if it turns out that nothing changes health-wise, but that the appointments are more convenient because people don't been to get childcare or leave work early, we can keep it. And not only can we use the variation to compare outcomes, the smaller scale means that we can try things out without messing up the whole country if it doesn't work.

Discussion Questions

1. What are some of the variables you think should be taken into consideration when comparing states on health outcomes? Why?
2. What are some hypotheses you could come up with to explain the variation in whether restaurants are allowed to be open, open at a reduced capacity or not open at all?
3. Is KFF a credible source? Why or why not? How do you know?
4. What are some of the drawbacks to having these "laboratories of democracy"?

Key Concepts

- Comparative method
- Laboratories of democracy
- Variance

For More Information:

https://www.oxfordreference.com/view/10.1093/oi/authority.20110803100232220
https://www.kff.org/

Note

1 One must be careful when it comes to these borders in modern Kansas City. For example, the author has a friend—let's call him Jeff. A few years ago, Jeff and his fiancé Judy (also a fake name) went to the courthouse on the Kansas side of Kansas City to get their marriage license. They had a beautiful ceremony (the author can personally attest to this) in a park near their house and hosted a raucous good time at the reception afterward. Fast forward a few months when they realized that they had never received their official marriage certificate like they had expected. When they contacted the county they were shocked to find out that the park in which they had had their ceremony was located in Missouri. As they had not been licensed to marry in Missouri, they were not actually married. They were able to go to the courthouse and be legally wed by the Justice of the Peace and it is all funny stories and two anniversaries now, however if they had not discovered the mistake and had there been a medical or financial emergency they might have been in for a world of issues. Borders matter.

Works Cited

Allison, D. (2020). *New 2020 Fortune 500 list has two big changes for Georgia companies.* Atlanta Business Chronicle. https://www.bizjournals.com/atlanta/news/2020/05/19/georgia-companies-on-2020-fortune-500-list.html

Cohn, S. (2019, July 10). *The comeback state of 2019: Kansas economy rebounds from tax-cutting disaster.* CNBC. https://www.cnbc.com/2019/07/09/top-state-mover-kansas-rebounds-from-tax-cutting-disaster.html

Georgia Historical Society. (n.d.). *Oglethorpe as a Georgia trustee.* Georgia Historical Society. Retrieved October 12, 2020, from https://georgiahistory.com/education-outreach/online-exhibits/featured-historical-figures/james-edward-oglethorpe/oglethorpe-georgias-trustee/

Georgia Humanities. (2009). *How the invention of Georgia's cotton gin changed the world.* Georgia Humanities. https://www.georgiahumanities.org/2016/12/07/how-the-invention-of-georgias-cotton-gin-changed-the-world/

Hall Family Foundation. (2019, January 29). *Forward progress to end the economic border war.* Hall Family Foundation. https://www.hallfamilyfoundation.org/whats-new/forward-progress-end-economic-border-war/

KFF. (2020) *State Data and Policy Actions to Address Coronavirus.* https://www.kff.org/coronavirus-covid-19/issue-brief/state-data-and-policy-actions-to-address-coronavirus/#policyactions

Langsdorf, E. (1950). A Review of Early Navigation on the Kansas River. Kansas Historical Society. https://www.kshs.org/p/a-review-of-early-navigation-on-the-kansas-river/13091

New Georgia Encyclopedia. (2018a). *Great depression.* New Georgia Encyclopedia. https://www.georgiaencyclopedia.org/articles/history-archaeology/great-depression

New Georgia Encyclopedia. (2018b). *State flags of Georgia.* New Georgia Encyclopedia. https://www.georgiaencyclopedia.org/articles/government-politics/state-flags-georgia

New Georgia Encyclopedia. (2017). *Slavery in Antebellum Georgia.* New Georgia Encyclopedia. https://www.georgiaencyclopedia.org/articles/history-archaeology/slavery-antebellum-georgia

New State Ice Company v. Liebmann, (U.S. 1932).

Prokop, A. (2014, July 8). *How Sam Brownback's tax cuts backfired.* Vox. https://www.vox.com/2014/7/8/5868717/sam-brownback-kansas-tax-cut

Tabuchi, H., & Fountain, H. (2017, June 1). Bucking Trump, These Cities, States and Companies Commit to Paris Accord. *The New York Times.* https://www.nytimes.com/2017/06/01/climate/american-cities-climate-standards.html

U.S. Census Bureau. (1983). *Census Tracts: Census of Population and Housing.* https://www2.census.gov/prod2/decennial/documents/1980/tracts-states/CensusTracts1980-Georgia.pdf

U.S. Census Bureau. (2019). Quick Facts: Georgia. https://www.census.gov/quickfacts/GA.

Zainaldin, J. (2017). *Before Hartsfield-Jackson, building bombers transformed the metro area's economy.* SaportaReport. https://saportareport.com/hartsfield-jackson-building-bombers-transformed-metro-areas-economy.

2

FEDERALISM AND INTERGOVERNMENTAL RELATIONS

The United States is somewhat usual in that by design its subnational governments—especially states—are assigned a central domestic policymaking role and are supposed to enjoy a high degree of independence from the central government. This importance and independence are products of federalism. Federalism is a political system in which the national and regional governments share powers and are considered independent equals. This system of shared powers is critical to understanding the politics of states and localities, and the central role they play in the U.S. political system. The question at the heart of it all is: who—the federal government or the state governments—has the power to do what?

We explore that question in this chapter in three ways. The first section is a disaster—or at least it is about disasters. The U.S. is huge and covers several topographical and weather zones. As such, we see a wide variety of natural disasters, from earthquakes to tornados to floods to blizzards. It is expensive to bail out after these things happen, and the relationships between localities and states and the federal government come into play here. The next section looks at the federal ownership of land. Many people understand that the federal government controls things like natural parks and monuments but outside of the west it isn't necessarily common knowledge that the federal government owns so much land. Here we discuss the reasons why this is the case and some of the issues and controversies that come along with it. Finally, we take a look at the United States Department of Education, one of the more controversial federal agencies. Their Office of Civil Rights is charged with ensuring that the nation's schools are compliant with civil rights laws, which is both an important and difficult job.

Hurricanes, Floods, and Tornados Oh My!
The High Cost of Disaster Recovery

The capacity to grant money gives the federal government a considerable amount of power over state and local governments. The ability to choose who gets the money and what they have to spend it on is a powerful one indeed. The federal government provides state and local governments more than $700B (Congressional Research Service 2019) in federal grants these days, funding a wide range of public policies such as environmental initiatives, social services, education, healthcare, transportation, and community and economic development, among many others.

The federal government allocates grants to state and local governments in one of two ways, either based on formulas established by law or through a competitive process (this is generally used for special projects). Even within the grants that are based on formulas, there are two different ways that the federal government does this: block grants and categorical grants.

Block grants consist of money given for a broad purpose with few strings attached, while categorical grants are given for a more specific purpose and have more restrictions about how the money is spent. Think of it this way, if I give you $20 and tell you to go to the store to buy supplies for dinner that is like a block grant. I gave you a general purpose, dinner, but didn't give you any specifics beyond that. If I gave you the same $20 and told you to buy hamburger, buns, ketchup, pickles, and a bag of fries, that would be more like a categorical grant. You still have some room to make choices (Rally's fries over Ore-Ida? Go for it! You want to save money by getting the generic ketchup rather than the fancy Heinz ketchup so that you can spring for the good seeded buns? Good for you!), but you are certainly more limited than you were under the block grant for groceries.

Which of these is favored by the federal government changes depending on who is in charge at any given time. When the administration feels the need to exercise more control over state decision-making, categorical grants tend to be more common. When they feel like giving more power and responsibility back to the states, you see more block grants. For instance, many Republicans ran for Congress in 1994 on a platform of states' rights and independence. When they gained control of Congress in that year, they changed many of the federal grants from categorical to block. So, instead of giving money to states to buy computers and textbooks, they gave blocks of money to spend on "education" more broadly, however the states saw fit.

We could go back and forth forever about how much power or independence states should have from the federal government. Indeed, that debate has been going on pretty much continuously since our nation's founding. One area where this has come up repeatedly is with disaster relief.

Multiple federal agencies are involved in disaster relief and recovery, but it is the role of the Federal Emergency Management Agency (FEMA) that is the most visible. When a disaster happens and a state wants federal help, there is a process that they have to go through. This process is laid out by law—the Robert T. Stafford Disaster Relief and Emergency Assistance Act. Basically, the governor asks the president for aid. FEMA assesses the situation and makes a recommendation to the president who then decides whether to declare a disaster or emergency. Both of these things come with assistance, but how much varies based on the nature of the problem.

Once the president declares a disaster or emergency, FEMA can pay out funds in three areas, public assistance, individual assistance, and hazard mitigation. The public assistance category pays for things like infrastructure repair for roads and public utilities. Individual assistance is for things like housing and unemployment assistance for displaced people. Hazard mitigation funds preventing future disasters, so it might be allocated toward replacing levees, raising river banks, or even elevating houses. FEMA is allocated its own pot of money each year and congress can delegate relief money over and above the amount FEMA has, if the need arises.

In August of 2005, a Category 3 hurricane hit the Gulf Coast of the U.S, causing catastrophic damage all the way from the eastern shores of Texas around to central Florida. In Louisiana, there were 125 mile per hour winds and up to fifteen inches of rain fell on parts of the state. Storm surge off of the ocean was measured at more than fourteen feet in areas of the coast and Lake Ponchartraine spilled over its banks causing significant flooding as well. Around 900,000 Louisianans lost power. In some of the hardest hit areas, such as St. Bernard Parish, more than 81% of the residential housing units were damaged or destroyed.

New Orleans was hit particularly hard, both by the hurricane itself and then a few days later when the flood protection levees failed and massive amounts of flood water rushed into the city and the surrounding parishes. Approximately 80% of the city flooded. Most of the major roads serving the city were damaged, including large portions of the Twin Span Bridge on I-10, which collapsed. All told, more than 1500 people died in Louisiana, most of them in New Orleans and St. Bernard Parish (Cook and Rosenberg 2015).

Louisiana's total budget for 2005 was $17.5 billion (Hines and Bajoie 2004) and New Orleans was working with an operating budget of around $750 million (City of New Orleans 2005). The damage from Hurricane Katina cost over $125 billion (National Oceanic and Atmospheric Administration 2017). This doesn't even include the economic impact of an area that relies very heavily on tourism. According to an estimate by Professor Bernard Weinstein of the University of North Texas, the damage and economic impact combined add up to closer to $250 billion (Amadeo 2008). Even though spending money on disaster relief is an example of a concurrent power, something that the states and the federal government can do, Louisiana doesn't have that kind of money. Remember that other than Vermont, states can't borrow money and practice deficit spending, and this is not something that they can scrape together in a pinch. But you know who can come up with that amount? The federal government.

Elected officials holding the political position that the federal government shouldn't be involved in state business, including emergency relief has not been uncommon over the years, but neither has changing that position after disaster strikes. In the mid-1960s, Louisiana governor John McKeithen had been running with a "federal government is the enemy" narrative for several years. After the Brown v. Board of Education ruling and then again after the passage of the Civil Rights Act and the Voting Rights Act, he had admitted that Louisiana had seriously considered seceding from the Union again. Soon after though, in September of 1965, Hurricane Betsy struck the Gulf Coast, killing more than 70 people and becoming the first hurricane to cause over a billion dollars' worth of damage. This presented a problem for Governor McKeithen. How do you reconcile keeping the federal government out of your business with desperately needing their help? McKeithen changed his tune on the usefulness of the federal government, expressing gratitude for the funding and admitting that those in D.C. were "the only people we can look to for the tremendous amount of money" (Horowitz 2012).

A similar situation happened in New Jersey in 2012, when Chris Christie, a self-proclaimed states' rights Republican embraced the federal government's help after Superstorm Sandy struck the Eastern Seaboard of the U.S. New Jersey was heavily damaged, as Sandy flooded major cities like Hoboken and Atlantic City and washed away beaches and boardwalks all along the coast. 43 people died and almost $40 billion worth of damage was done in New Jersey alone (Horowitz 2012). Governor Christie has been an outspoken figure on this topic ever since, criticizing other Republican leaders for what he perceives as hypocrisy as they ask for disaster relief from the same federal government that they lambast the rest of the time.

Luckily for everyone in the states that have been struck by disaster, as Governor McKeithen put it back in 1965, "when we got in trouble ... no suggestion was made, 'Well, you people have been talking down there about states' rights. You can take care of your own problems.'"

Discussion Questions

1. Why should taxpayers in Montana have to pay for people to live in Florida where there are hurricanes all the time?
2. Is it hypocritical for a politician to tout state's rights and independence from the federal government and then to take federal money after a disaster?
3. Which would be better in an emergency, a block grant or a categorical grant? Why?

Key Concepts

*   Federalism
*   Concurrent powers
*   Categorical grants
*   Block grants

For More Information:

https://www.fema.gov/disaster-declaration-process
https://www.fema.gov/media-library/assets/documents/15271
https://fas.org/sgp/crs/homesec/R43537.pdf
https://www.politifact.com/truth-o-meter/article/2017/sep/14/how-us-funds-disaster-recovery/

Federal Ownership of Land, or, When Nevada isn't Actually Nevada

At 3.67 million square miles, the United States is a very large country. It is the third largest country in the world, in terms of land mass—only Russia and Canada are bigger. Because of how our federal system of government is set up, this giant chunk of land is divided up into 50 states. America's founders designed this system purposely in order to preserve regional culture, protect individual rights, and prevent a too-powerful federal government from taking over. A map of the U.S. contains clear divisions, borders between states, some that run along the lines of naturally occurring landmarks like rivers or lakes, and some that were simply drawn by people.

Those lines are important. Kill someone during a robbery in Walla Walla, Washington? You are looking at life in prison as a punishment. Pretty harsh, but if you do the same thing over the border in Pendleton, Oregon, you might be facing the death penalty. This is a big difference, no? The sovereignty that states enjoy over many of the goings on, including deciding how to punish criminals that commit state crimes, is enshrined in the Constitution of the United States.

It turns out that states don't have control over all of the land inside of their states though. In fact, some states don't have control over large portions of the land inside of their borders—the federal government does. Well sure, you might say, National Parks belong to the country, not to the state where it is located. And it is true, National Parks are one of times that land is managed by the federal government rather than by the state, but the parks only make up a small part of the giant swaths of federally controlled land.

The federal government controls about 28% of the land in the United States. At over 1 million square miles[1] (Congressional Research Service 2019), this is so much land that if it were a country in and of itself, it would be the 30th largest country in the world, larger than places like Egypt, Venezuela, Pakistan, and France. This ownership is not spread out evenly though, ranging from only .3% of the land in Iowa and Connecticut to almost 80% of the land in Nevada. The western states have far higher concentrations of federal land; 46.4% of the land in the coterminous western states and 61.3% of the land in Alaska are under federal control. This is highly controversial, but we will get to that in a minute.

First, some history. Back before the United States united, several of the colonies had claimed land to the west of their main borders. When they tossed the Articles of Confederation out the window and gave authority to the new central government with the signing of the new U.S. Constitution one of the things that they had to do was give up their rights to this "western" land (I use quotes here because what they considered western at the time was between the Appalachian mountains and Mississippi river, much of which currently lies in the Eastern time zone). The federal government now had the constitutional ability to regulate land to the west of the original states and to create new states.

Over the next hundred years or so, numerous laws were passed dealing with this land. Congress passed legislation to encourage people to move west and settle the land. The Homestead Act of 1862 and the Desert Lands Entry Act of 1877 are two such examples. More than 1.25B acres of land was transferred from federal ownership to private by 1940. The federal government gave or sold land to individuals, businesses (often railroads and other businesses that were doing things deemed to be in the public interest), and to the states themselves. The federal government was largely in the business of divesting itself of these huge swaths of land that they didn't really want to manage. They weren't able to get rid of all of it, however. A lot of the land in the western half of the United States is not really suited for homesteading; there are a lot of mountains and deserts and rocks and a notable lack of water.

The United States was developing so quickly that there was also a growing concern that we were going to mess up some of America's beautiful scenery and natural resources. In response, a movement toward conservation and preservation gained ground. So, by having this land that was largely not suitable for things like farming and with the pressure created by these new conservation groups, the United States began reserving land—the first national parks were created, Yellowstone in 1872; Mackinac in 1885; Rock Creek, Yosemite, and Sequoia in 1890. We also started setting aside land as national forest preserves in the late 19th century. Of course, these parks and forests didn't take up all of the millions of acres of federal land, so the Bureau of Land Management was created to manage the land that was left.

By the time the 20th century was in full swing, the federal government had slowed their conveyance of land to private interests and state ownership considerably. And then in 1976, they enacted the Federal Land Policy and Management

Act (FLPMA) where they stated outright that the current federal lands would remain under federal ownership. No more homesteading. No more transferring land to the states. Unsurprisingly, this did not sit well with many people. Many states feel that most of that land should be under their control. Farmers and ranchers often have disagreements about federal rules and regulations regarding grazing lands. Some see these millions of acres as wasted opportunities for the excavation of resources or for development.

Many rural westerners began to struggle. Heavy restrictions and fees had been placed on the federal lands, increasing the burden on activities like mining, ranching, and logging. Limits on the number of cattle allowed to graze in certain areas and decreased speed limits proved extremely unpopular with many, and in response, some of the opponents began to organize, adopting the name "Sagebrush Rebellion" after the plant common in many of the western states. In 1979, the Nevada legislature passed a bill claiming rights over 49 million acres of public land within its borders. This was largely symbolic as the federal government had made it clear that they had no intention of turning over this land, but Nevada's act, though legally meaningless, created more attention and support for the movement. Congressional delegates from the western states actively and proudly identified themselves as sagebrush rebels. Even Ronald Reagan expressed his support and solidarity during a visit to Utah.

After his election, President Reagan, though he could not unitarily overturn the FLPMA, did what he could from the Executive Branch. He and his Interior Secretary James Watt created and instituted the Good Neighbor Policy. This policy gave western lawmakers and land users more representation in the decisions that were being made about land use and management at the department level. This move helped placate the Sagebrush Rebels for a while, but the conflict between the federal government and many of these westerners is still salient.

In January of 2016, a group of heavily armed militants took over the office building at the Malheur National Wildlife Refuge in Harney County, Oregon. They occupied the building for over a month, until February 11, 2016. The organizers, a group of ranchers, members of the sovereign citizen movement, and various other non-governmental militias, were ostensibly protesting federal control over western lands. Specifically, they were angry that two local ranchers had been convicted of arson on federal lands and took the position that the land shouldn't have been federal in the first place. The group, led by a man named Ammon Bundy, took up arms and occupied the wildlife refuge's headquarters.

By the time the last arrest was made in February, more than two dozen of the occupiers had been arrested and charged with federal offenses and one man had been shot and killed after he reached for a gun while trying to go through a roadblock. The occupation had the effect of renewing the public attention to the federal land ownership issue. Various stakeholders and interested groups came forward to make statements both in support of the militants (though many criticized their tactics) and to condemn them. Considering the vehemence seen in this group's beliefs and the support seen by many for their sentiment, if not for their actions, it is unlikely that we have seen the end of this debate.

Discussion Questions

1. Is it in the U.S.'s best interest that the government own so much land, especially in the west? Why or why not?
2. What other scenarios can you imagine in which there might be a conflict between the federal and state governments over federal land ownership?
3. Does the "Good Neighbor Policy" seem like a sufficient way to alleviate the tension between the federal government and public land users?
4. To what extent is it the federal government's responsibility to balance things like recreation, agricultural use, resource extraction, and preservation on these lands? What interests should be favored?

Key Concepts

- Federalism
- State Sovereignty
- Bureau of Land Management
- Federal Land Policy and Management Act

For More Information:

https://www.loc.gov/collections/ranching-culture-in-northern-nevada-from-1945-to-1982/articles-and-essays/a-history-of-the-ninety-six-ranch/the-sagebrush-rebellion-1960-1982/
https://fas.org/sgp/crs/misc/R42346.pdf

FedEd: Investigating Civil Rights Violations in Schools

When people think about laws and policies, they often look to the federal government for guidance. After all, the Supremacy Clause in the Constitution says that the Constitution and the federal laws made to support it carry the weight as the supreme law of the land and that state courts are bound to its authority. But there are some areas of law that were specifically designated to the states and the founders made clear that if they hadn't listed something specifically in the Constitution that it too should be reserved for the states to handle.

One such area is education policy. There is no mention of education in the Constitution, and the 10th Amendment makes it clear that this means that it should be a function of the states. Thus, school districts are funded and run by state and local governments.

One of the outcomes of this system is that there is some pretty significant variation between states and sometimes even within states as to what you can expect at school. For instance, in Arizona "a pupil must correctly answer at least 60 of the 100 questions listed on a test that is identical to the civics portion of the naturalization test used by the United States citizenship and immigration services" (Arizona Office of Education 2016) in order to graduate, while next door in Nevada, there is no testing requirement in civics or government at all (Education Commission of the States 2016).

There is variation in quality as well. New York spends more than $20,000 per student per year on instruction and support services, while Utah only spends around $7,000. This is not a problem in and of itself, nor is it something that the federal government directly concerns itself with. States can fund their education systems pretty much as they please. And after all, there is a considerable difference in the cost of living between Utah and New York.

Sometimes variations such as the above matters though, and that is when the federal government keeps an eye on things. Take the SATs, for example. Students in Massachusetts and Connecticut have far higher average SAT scores than students in Alabama and West Virginia—more than 250 points higher (World Population Review 2020). Massachusetts and Connecticut also spend far more money per pupil on education than Alabama and West Virginia. Massachusetts and Connecticut also emphasize college readiness and test preparation more than the average state. Does this mean that the students in Alabama and West Virginia are getting shortchanged? Maybe. And in some cases, the federal government tells a state that they have to spend more money or change their curriculum or requirements to make sure that the needs of students are being met.

The federal government didn't issue any educational policy at all until the 1960s, when the National Science Foundation published a report looking at the relative effectiveness of different educational techniques. Since then, federal involvement in education has increased substantially, largely in the areas of equal access and equal protection. Spending on education makes up only about 3% of the federal budget, but this adds up to billions of dollars. Most of the money is used for assistance for students with disabilities and to administer the assessment known as the Nation's Report Card, however some of the money is spent to specifically protect the rights of the students and teachers in the nation's schools. Even though education isn't a directly protected constitutional right, it is considered so important that we pay very close attention to the constitutional rights of those in the system.

To try to achieve that goal, the U.S. Department of Education has a subagency called the Office for Civil Rights whose job it is to enforce the civil rights laws that prohibit discrimination based on race, color, national origin (Title VI of the Civil Rights Act of 1964), sex (Title IX of the Education Amendments of 1972), disability (Section 504 of the Rehabilitation Act of 1973), age (Age Discrimination Act of 1975), or membership in patriotic youth organizations (Boy Scouts of America Equal Access Act of 2001).

In April of 2017, the OCR gave notice that it was opening an investigation into the Richmond, VA public school district. The notice alleged complaints of disciplinary policies and practices that unlawfully discriminate against African American students and students with disabilities. The investigation was based on a complaint filed the previous August by the Legal Aid Justice Center and the ACLU of Virginia on behalf of two individual students, alleging that the discipline policies in place in the Richmond Public Schools effectively punished African American students and students with disabilities more harshly and more frequently than their peers.

The complaint alleges that during the 2014-15 school year, African American students with disabilities were almost thirteen times more likely than white students without disabilities to face short-term suspension as a punishment. Further, according to Virginia Department of Education data, more than 90% of the nearly 5,000 students suspended during the 2015-16 school year in the Richmond Public School district were black, even though they make up only 74% of the student population. Students with disabilities comprise about 18% of the student population but more than 37% of those students who were suspended.

When the OCR investigates complaints like this one, they take the allegations and their implications very seriously. They spend time collecting and analyzing information from the complainants and any witnesses that may have information about what happened. They also collect information from the school and school district, looking closely at the policies and procedures that are in place and how those get interpreted and implemented in classrooms.

This is such an in-depth process that as of this writing the investigation is still ongoing. This can be incredibly frustrating for everyone involved, but considering the gravity of the complaints handled by the OCR, it is appropriate that they are diligent and measured in their investigation. This is especially true considering the potential outcomes for a school or district can be pretty significant.

There are a few different ways that these investigations can go. The OCR can dismiss a complaint. They usually do this if the complainant doesn't have standing or if the complaint wasn't filed properly. If they do open an investigation, a lot of times they are able to facilitate an agreement between the parties. So, the school will agree to change a policy or to give a student a service or something. If this goes according to plan and all of the parties, including the OCR, are happy with the outcome, they can close the file and call the issue resolved. If this doesn't happen and the OCR has to carry the investigation out to its completion, they can find either that the entity did violate policy or that they didn't. If the finding is that there was no violation, the case is closed. If they do find that there was a violation though, the OCR has to enforce the policy and get the entity to remedy the problem. Because the OCR isn't a court of law or even a police department, a lot of this depends of the compliance of the school or district to voluntarily comply and fix the problems that the OCR found. And if they don't (which is pretty rare), the OCR may take them to court and sue them.

The power that the OCR has to compel schools and school districts to act in a particular way on certain topics can really irritate some people. After all, shouldn't education stay in the realm of the states? But equal access to education is something that we as a society have decided we value, and protection from discrimination is a federal issue. Considering there are almost 7,000 open cases in various stages of investigation at the OCR, it seems that perhaps oversight of these areas is important.

Discussion Questions

1. What is the argument against having a Federal Department of Education? Do you find the argument valid? Why or why not?
2. Why does the federal government help pay for accommodations for students with disabilities? How is this a civil rights issue?
3. If an investigation is going to take years and years to complete, should any teachers involved be placed on leave? Why or why not?

Key Concepts

- Federalism
- Supremacy Clause
- Variance
- Nation's Report Card
- Department of Education Office of Civil Rights

For More Information:

https://www2.ed.gov/about/offices/list/ocr/index.html
https://www.npr.org/2019/10/19/769555063/key-changes-would-alter-the-governments-massive-survey-on-schools-and-civil-righ
https://er.educause.edu/blogs/2018/12/the-department-of-educations-office-of-civil-rights-reverses-course-on-mass-filer-civil-rights

Note

1 Oddly enough, we are not sure exactly how much land is controlled by the federal government. We can estimate based on the records of the agencies that manage the land, but that estimate is pretty rough. We also tend not to count Indian lands that are held in trust by the federal government or things like marine refuges or subterranean interests.

Works Cited

Amadeo, K. (2008, September 1). *Hurricane Katrina Facts, Damage, and Costs*. The Balance; The Balance. https://www.thebalance.com/hurricane-katrina-facts-damage-and-economic-effects-3306023

Arizona Office of Education. (2016, January 6). *Civics Education*. Office of Education, Office of the Arizona Governor. https://education.azgovernor.gov/edu/civics-education

City of New Orleans, Louisiana. (2005). *City of New Orleans Basic Financial Statements (With Independent Auditors' Report Thereon)*. https://www.nola.gov/accounting/files/comprehensive-annual-financial-report/2005-final-audit-report/

Congressional Research Service. (2019). *Federal Grants to State and Local Governments: A Historical Perspective on Contemporary Issues*. https://fas.org/sgp/crs/misc/R40638.pdf

Cook, L., & Rosenberg, E. (2015). *No One Knows How Many People Died in Katrina*. US News & World Report; U.S. News & World Report. https://www.usnews.com/news/blogs/data-mine/2015/08/28/no-one-knows-how-many-people-died-in-katrina

Education Commission of the States. (2016). *Civic Education Policies: State Profile*. http://ecs.force.com/mbdata/mbstcprofancg?rep=CIP16ST&st=Nevada

Hines, D., & Bajoie, D. (2004). *FY 2005 State Budget Highlights Louisiana State Senate*. http://senate.legis.state.la.us/fiscalservices/Publications/FY04-05/FY05StateHighlights/FY05StateHighlights.pdf

Horowitz, A. (2012, November 2). *Lessons in the Glory of Federal Power From 1965's Hurricane Betsy*. Slate Magazine. https://slate.com/news-and-politics/2012/11/sandy-and-chris-christie-lessons-from-hurricane-betsy-in-1965.html

National Oceanic and Atmospheric Administration. (2017). *Hurricane Costs*. noaa.Gov. https://coast.noaa.gov/states/fast-facts/hurricane-costs.html

World Population Review. (2020). *SAT Scores by State 2020*. worldpopulationreview.com. https://worldpopulationreview.com/state-rankings/sat-scores-by-state

3
STATE CONSTITUTIONS

State constitutions have an enormous impact on state governments and policymaking—and on us. They affect the education we receive, the employment opportunities we enjoy, the political culture of the states in which we live, and the rights we do (or don't have). State constitutions and the rights and powers they provide also vary widely.

In recent years, state constitutions have become more important, not less. Since the 1990s, the U.S. Supreme Court has handed down a number of decisions, some of which have strengthened state governments at the expense of the federal government and others that have trumped state law. State courts are also becoming more assertive. In 1977, Supreme Court justice William Brennan, a former NJ state supreme court justice, wrote an article for the Harvard Law Review that noted that state constitutions afford their citizens another layer of right above and beyond the rights afforded by the U.S. Constitution. He urged state courts to pay more attention to this responsibility … and they have.

We start here with a topic that will resonate with some of you reading this and will seem completely foreign to others, the right to hunt and fish. These activities have long been tradition around the U.S., both as a hobby/sport and as a means for acquiring food. Considering the move over the last 40 years or so toward protecting animals, some hunting advocates worry that their activity may be in danger. That's where state constitutions have stepped in. Next, we move to a more urban area, Euclid, OH. Euclid is facing some challenges as a city and some have suggested that the state step in to help. The twist here is that the Ohio state constitution may prohibit the state from doing that, even if it means that Euclid doesn't get the help it needs. We cap this chapter off by talking about preemption laws. From trash bags to gun control, it is becoming more and more common for states to tell cities that they aren't allowed to pass certain kinds of legislation. We look closer at why this is and what it means.

The Right to Hunt and Fish and Hang Out on the Front Porch

On Election Day in 2018, by a 14-point margin, North Carolina voters approved an amendment to their state constitution codifying their right to hunt and fish. While this amendment in North Carolina garnered some attention (though it was overshadowed by some other issues that came up in this particular election in North Carolina), amendments such as this one are not new. More than 20 states have added provisions like this one to their constitutions, limiting states' power to regulate hunting and establishing hunting as the predominate method of wildlife management.

If you don't follow the latest in hunting or wildlife management news, you might wonder whether or not these amendments are necessary. The hunting community says yes. In fact, they point out, there were two separate cases in 2018 that illustrate why state-level constitutional amendments are necessary—both having to do with bears—in New Jersey and Yellowstone National Park.

Black bear hunting has been outlawed in New Jersey since the 1950s when the population of the bears dropped to record lows. Over the next few decades, the bear population rebounded, and in the early 2000s, people started talking about bringing back the hunt. In 2003, the New Jersey Fish and Game Council authorized the first black bear hunt in half a century and scheduled one for that year and another for 2005.

Anti-hunting groups filed a lawsuit before the 2005 hunt, effectively preventing it from happening, and in 2006, the state Supreme Court ruled that the Fish and Game Council could not schedule these hunts because they didn't have a black bear management plan. Ok, this was a pretty easy fix, so they developed a plan and in 2010, with the five-year management plan in place, the bear hunts returned.

The black bear population had increased steadily since the 1950s, and by the mid-2010s, there was estimated to be more than 3,500 in the northwestern part of the state (the location of the hunt). Because the population was doing well, when the management plan was renewed in 2015, a second hunt was added to the year.

Of course, people who were against bear hunting when there was only one hunt a year were not happy with this development, and when Phil Murphy was running for governor, he promised some of the anti-hunting groups that he would ban the hunts completely. Murphy did end up winning the governorship and did attempt to make good on his campaign promise, however it turns out that his ability to do so was limited by law. While he was not able to ban the bear hunts completely, he was able to prohibit bear hunting on lands owned or managed by the state Department of Environmental Protection, including state parks, state forests, and wildlife management areas.

More than 2,000 miles to the west lives a different type of bear. Back when Lewis and Clark were trekking across the continent, there were more than 50,000 grizzly bears roaming around the Rocky Mountains and Great Plains, however by the time they were listed as a federally threatened species in 1975, there were fewer than 500 living in this area and only 136 in the greater Yellowstone National Park ecosystem (U.S. Fish and Wildlife Services 2012).

Landing on the Endangered List meant a few things for these bears. The Interagency Grizzly Bear Study Team was formed to coordinate bear monitoring and research among the various federal and state agencies that do that sort of thing. The Interagency Grizzly Bear Committee was also formed to increase cooperation and communication among the levels of management in the recovery areas and to create public education programs. Finally, and most importantly for this article, the grizzly bear hunting season stopped.

Since becoming a federally protected species, the grizzly bear population has recovered significantly. So much so, in fact, that the federal Fish and Wildlife Service removed the bears in the Yellowstone area from the protected list in 2017, arguing that the current numbers were slightly above the sustainable population numbers for the area.

As in New Jersey, not everyone was happy with this turn of events and a coalition of more than twenty groups—environmentalists, Native tribes, and conservation groups, brought a lawsuit against the Fish and Wildlife Service in an attempt to keep the bears on the protected list. It worked (at least for now) and in 2018, a U.S. District Judge restored protections for the Yellowstone-area population of grizzly bears under the Endangered Species Act. No grizzly bear hunting in the greater Yellowstone area for the time being.

So, maybe hunters have a reason to be worried. After all there are two high-profile instances of increased restrictions on hunting just in 2018. Further, it seems that Americans are becoming increasingly sympathetic to animals. According to PEW research, Americans have become increasingly opposed to the use of animals in scientific research, more likely to live a vegetarian or vegan lifestyle, and yes, less likely to hunt or support hunting (Strauss 2018). In fact, only about a third of U.S. gun owners hunt at all (Mitchell 2017).

Some argue though that the right to hunt and fish is not really at risk at all and the push for amendments like these are nothing but a political ploy to bring conservative voters to the polls. The NRA's American Hunter website is pretty explicit in their intent to use the issue to increase favorable voter turnout. They use discourse about the eroding rights of hunters to pursue their activity, "every day, actually every hour, animal-rights extremists, and supposedly well-meaning but ill-informed people in the United States and across the globe, are working to end hunting" (National Rifle Association 2018). They then acknowledge that while they might not be able to convince activists that hunting is a good thing that if hunters turn out at the polls and bring all of their friends and family to the polls as well that more candidates who support the Second Amendment will win races.

The American Civil Liberties Union advised voting against the North Carolina amendment, arguing that it does nothing but clutter up the state's most important document. They point out that there is very little explanation for the need for the amendment and that even some of the legislators who supported the bill had admitted that it wasn't necessary. They also point out that the language of the amendment is worded nearly exactly like the model legislation written by the NRA.

This is not the first time someone has accused hunting rights advocates of cluttering up a state constitution. In 2005, when a similar amendment was proposed in Nebraska, state senator Ernie Chambers introduced a whole host of amendments, both in an attempt to kill it and to try to make a point about adding things to the state constitution. The amendments would have had the Nebraska Constitution protecting such things as "creating, recreating, conversating, and procreating", "hunting for the link between Noah's Ark, Joan of Arc, and Archimedes" and "sitting on the front porch on a warm summer evening, drinking a glass of cold lemonade, dreamily watching the silvery moon rise to begin its journey across a darkening velvet sky powdered with stardust" (Catania 2006).

It might have been a silly way to make a point, but Chambers stood by it, saying that it is just as silly to think that the state would ever ban hunting and fishing. And while the Governor of New Jersey works to restrict black bear hunting and a federal judge keeps hunters from taking grizzlies, perhaps Chambers was right. While there are restrictions on hunting and fishing designed to protect animal and human populations, there is no evidence of a serious move toward any more widespread bans on the activities. Or perhaps he was wrong and these laws are necessary, not for now, but for the future.

Discussion Questions

1. What topics do you consider so important that they should be included in state constitutions rather than simply codified in state law?
2. Who should be in charge of deciding what animals need protection?
3. How should elected officials balance hunting with species sustainability?
4. What is the risk that comes with putting too many items into a state constitution?

Key Concepts

- Constitution
- Amendment

For More Information:

https://www.ncleg.gov/Sessions/2017/Bills/Senate/PDF/S677v5.pdf
https://www.sosnc.gov/static_forms/NC_Constitutional_Documents/2018/
S677_Official_Explanation.pdf
http://www.ncsl.org/research/environment-and-natural-resources/state-
constitutional-right-to-hunt-and-fish.aspx

Problems in Euclid and the Limitations of the Ohio Constitution

If you simply go by the U.S. Constitution, only the federal and state governments have any sovereign authority. Cities, counties, towns, special districts, and
the like simply don't exist except as creations of the states wherein they reside.
Thus, it is a function of state constitutions to figure out to what extent, if any,
these administrative subdivisions have authority to self-govern.

Local governments in the U.S. generally follow one of two models, Dillon's
Rule or Home Rule. Dillon's Rule is the default and Home Rule must be established by the state (and has been in most states). Dillon's Rule, which originated
in the Iowa State Supreme Court and was upheld by the U.S. Supreme Court,
asserts that because local governments are political and administrative subdivisions of the state, they exist to perform the tasks of the state at the local level. In
other words, local government's power is derived by the state and is thus limited
to what the state says it can do. Generally, the states that abide by Dillon's Rule
do delegate some power to local governments in areas such as planning, zoning,
and some areas of taxation—areas where it is effective for the governance to exist
where it is closest to the people that it will affect.

Some localities argue that they should have more sovereignty and be seen as
a legitimate and separate level of authority. That is where Home Rule comes in.
In 1875, Missouri passed the first Home Rule charter. This was quickly followed
by similar legislation in California, Minnesota, and Washington. Since then, 44
states have adopted some form of Home Rule. Under these laws, localities can
exercise some autonomous authority without worrying about state interference.
There is variation here—for example Illinois has Home Rule for cities that have
a population over 25,000, while North Dakota has Home Rule for all cities.

In Ohio, cities and towns are granted Home Rule by Article XVIII of the
Ohio Constitution. This section reads: "Municipalities shall have authority to

exercise all powers of local self-government and to adopt and enforce within their limits such local police, sanitary, and other similar regulations, as are not in conflict with general laws" (Ohio Legislature 2017).

This clause has been further specified by the courts to mean that the state of Ohio cannot interfere in a locality's internal organization, zoning and property usage rules, employment and salaries of elected officials and municipal employees, and the authority to pass regulations regarding the health, safety, and morals of society. In other words, Ohio's state officials cannot step in and tell a city what to do in these areas and can, in fact, only interfere on matters that are of statewide interest.

Home Rule can be great in so many ways. Sometimes government that is closer to the people who live there can be more responsive, and more appropriately responsive simply because of proximity. The needs of one city in one area of a state might not be the same as those of a different city in a different area. Home Rule gives municipalities more flexibility to tax their citizens and to decide what to do with those taxes. Cities often have a better understanding of their staffing and policing needs than the central state government, and Home Rule can allow them the ability to act accordingly. There is a downside too, however. And we can see an example of this down side in Euclid, Ohio.

Euclid, Ohio is a suburb of Cleveland. The third largest suburb, Euclid has just under 50,000 residents. It lies along the shore of Lake Erie and boasts the National Cleveland-Style Polka Hall of Fame, the headquarters of the Lincoln Electric Company, and one of the top ranked libraries in the country for a city of its size. There is a lovely golf course, a fishing pier, an ice arena … many of the things that people like when they are looking for a place to live.

Not everything is all rainbows and sunshine in Euclid though. Since the 1970s, the population has dropped from over 70,000 and between 2005 and 2015 the poverty rate increased from 9.7% to almost 22% (U.S. Census Bureau 2019). The public works and infrastructure are aging, and problems like broken water mains and potholes the size of small ponds are common. Only about half of the available housing in Euclid is currently occupied. Businesses and industry have fled for neighboring communities. The school district recently received an F rating from the state and currently ranks close to the bottom of all of the districts in the state.

One of the things that happens when the population and business drops and poverty increases is that the tax revenue that a city depends on to, well, run itself decreases. Between 2005 and 2015, Euclid's tax base fell by over a quarter. And at the same time, the state of Ohio was decreasing state funding for things like local government support and public education. Euclid is facing a serious financial crisis. And because of the way Ohio's Home Rule works, Euclid is pretty much on its own to solve (or not solve) the problems that have resulted.

Euclid has certainly had its share of problems in recent years. In addition to some of woes that go along with a fiscal crisis (infrastructure, staffing, etc.),

Euclid has a bit of a police brutality problem. Between January of 2016 and June of 2018, there were 273 instances of use of force by officers documented (News 5 Cleveland 2018). This is really high for a city of this size. Even more concerning, a very high percentage of these incidents were committed by only a few officers.

Some of these cases have garnered national attention. In fact, Euclid was featured on the popular podcast, Serial, which looked at the (dis)function of the criminal justice system in Cuyahoga County, where Euclid is located. In addition to focusing a spotlight on a handful of the police brutality cases in Euclid, Serial also brought up another issue that is hanging over Euclid's administration: the fact that they are not paying on the judgements that have been made against them in some of these cases.

The city of Euclid has been sued many times over the alleged excessive use of police force and in several of these cases have lost. The courts have granted the plaintiffs monetary judgements to account for the damage done to them and their lives by the city, but many of these plaintiffs allege that they haven't been paid. One attorney familiar with the city even joked that if something happens to you in Euclid and they offer you a settlement, you should take it even if it is tiny because otherwise your chances of being paid, even if you win in court, are slim.

This gets even shadier when you look at who wins and who loses in Euclid. Most of the brutality cases and other issues with law enforcement involve the city's African American community. Many of these residents live in the inland neighborhoods, away from the lake. These neighborhoods tend to be more run down than the waterfront areas, more pot holes, fewer amenities, etc. But the neighborhoods closer to the water? Quite a bit of money has been invested over there in recent years. A new wharf area, newly paved roads, plenty of services. You get the picture. This is not a problem on its own, of course. Cities can choose where to spend their money, and it often makes sense to develop and improve attractive areas so that middle and upper class folks come and pay high property tax rates. It also helps bring businesses to your area. It is a problem though if a city is doing all of that, yet claiming that there isn't enough money to pay back victims of excessive police force per the judgements granted by a court of law.

This is a problem, but the state of Ohio can't do much about it because of the way their constitution is set up. Euclid is granted the right of Home Rule. They get to exercise this discretion broadly, even if the state doesn't like it. And this, of course, is the down side to Home Rule.

Discussion Questions

1. How does giving localities Home Rule benefit a state? What are the drawbacks?
2. In your opinion, how bad would the situation in a city have to be for it to be appropriate for a state to come and take over?

3. It is difficult to change a constitution. Would it be worth it for Ohio to reconsider and potentially try to change the Home Rule protections that they currently have because of problems like those seen in Euclid?

Key Concepts

- Constitution
- Self-government
- Sovereignty
- Dillon's Rule
- Home Rule

For More Information:

https://www.lsc.ohio.gov/documents/reference/current/membersonlybriefs/12 8municipalhomerule.pdf

https://www.alec.org/app/uploads/2016/01/2016-ACCE-White-Paper-Dillon-House-Rule-Final.pdf

From Plastic Bags to Guns: Preemption Laws and an Evolving Political Landscape

In March of 2013, the city of Austin, Texas passed a law banning single-use of plastic bags. A report presented to the Austin City Council by the Austin Resource Recovery and the Zero Waste Advisory Commission two years into the ban reported that Austinites had removed 50,000 pounds of plastic from the annual waste stream and reduced local bag use by 200,000,000 per years, achieving a 75% reduction in bag waste (Waters 2015). All told, eleven Texas cities passed similar ordinances, attempting to do their part to reduce the trash output and carbon footprint of their localities.

On June 22, 2018, the Texas Supreme Court shut those ordinances down. It turns out that Texas has a law (the 1993 Solid Waste Disposal Act) that prohibits municipalities from restricting the use of plastic bags. The state supreme court held that the state law overrides local rules that forbid retail provision of single-use bags at a point of sale.

Cities, as they stand per the U.S. Constitution, are devoid of any inherent power. The U.S. Constitution doesn't even mention local government, reserving any power not explicitly granted to the federal government to the state governments. The courts have largely upheld the subordinate nature of local governments, guided by Dillon's Rule. Starting way back in the late 1800s though, states started granting Home Rule powers to local governments, giving them more independence to self-govern without interference from the state.

Localities under Home Rule are still subject to preemption by the state, however Home Rule has served to significantly increase the power of cities and prevented states from interfering with many local activities. Until recently, there had been a trend favoring local control over many types of policies, but this has been changing.

There is definitely a partisan angle to the waxing and waning of states preempting local laws. During the Obama presidency, conservative advocacy groups like ALEC encouraged states to resist progressive policies by giving more control to local governments. This was made all the more powerful after the 2010 Supreme Court ruling in Citizens United v. FEC got rid of the restrictions on independent expenditures by corporations and may have given an advantage to Republican candidates. By 2011, Republicans had gained 675 seats in state legislatures, taking control of 25 state legislatures (up from fourteen the year prior) and gaining a trifecta (controlling the state house, senate, and governor's office) in 21 states (up from nine the previous year). Don't get me wrong, both major political parties have used state law to preempt local laws that they didn't like, but over the past decade or so, the preemption advantages have favored conservative policy. For example, 31 states prevent cities from creating rent-control policies to create affordable housing, 25 states block their cities from raising their minimum wage, and 23 states don't let their localities create paid sick leave laws.

One of the most controversial topics on which states have been seizing control from local governments is gun control. On August 4, 2019, a gunman killed nine people and injured an additional 27 in an entertainment district in Dayton, Ohio. He used an AR-15-style gun with a large capacity magazine. Prior to 2006, cities like Dayton, Columbus, Cincinnati, Toledo, and Cleveland had local-level assault weapons bans, but that year the state of Ohio passed H.B. 347, which prohibited localities from enacting their own gun bans. When the state passed that law, it effectually erased more than 80 local gun laws. The governor at the time, Bob Taft vetoed the bill, saying that it was detrimental to the tradition of Home Rule in Ohio, but the Ohio General Assembly voted to override the veto and the bill became law. It was upheld by the Ohio Supreme Court in 2010.

This is not to say that if Dayton still had an assault weapons ban the 2019 shooting wouldn't have happened. Of course, shootings continue to happen even in places with stricter gun laws. The discussion of the correlation between stricter gun regulations and gun violence is a whole other topic that we could spend pages and pages discussing, but that is for another time. For our purposes though, gun control laws make for an interesting example of how states have been increasing their use of preemption laws.

Ohio is only one of the 44 states that have laws that prohibit cities from creating gun control regulations. Typically, these laws say something like "all areas concerning firearms regulation" fall under the purview of the state and that municipal ordinances on any related topic are considered null and void. These laws have increased but this isn't a completely new thing. Way back in 1981, for example, Morton Grove, Illinois tried to pass a handgun ban, but the NRA and other gun groups sued and began to push for state preemption of local laws.

Historically, it was common for states to allow localities to make their own laws regarding guns. The primary reason for this is that it made sense to a lot of people to have different rules in urban and rural areas. For example, most schools do not allow any weapons on their property at any time for any reason, right? But what about rural areas where older teenagers go hunting in the early mornings before school and then go straight to campus with their hunting rifles still in their trucks? That may seem like a foreign concept to those of you who are reading this in urban or many suburban areas, but it is a pretty normal thing in many rural areas.

It is no coincidence that the vast majority of the gun-related preemption laws have been passed or strengthened since 2010. The conservative policy group, ALEC, has been pushing these laws, providing states with model bills for Republican lawmakers to introduce in their states. Similarly, the NRA has spent time lobbying for these laws and making large campaign donations to conservative lawmakers who support their efforts. Again, all made easier after the Citizens United ruling. They argue that it makes more sense to have a single, coherent law rather than a complex patchwork of local ordinances, a position that does make some sense. After all, it can be confusing to live in an area where driving a few blocks may mean that the law is different. On the other hand, mayors and city council members, especially in areas that have been hit hard by gun violence, can feel frustrated at their lack of ability to do anything about the problem.

The division of power between the Federal government and state governments, while it has become more complicated over time, is laid out in the U.S. constitution. The relationship between states and their municipalities is a far muddier one. Time will tell if states will continue to increase their preemption authority or if the pendulum will swing back the other way.

Discussion Questions

1. Why would Texas have a law that keeps cities from regulating plastic bag use? Who are the stakeholders here and why does it matter?
2. Considering that a majority of Americans are in favor of some version of gun control why would states restrict cities from implementing these policies?
3. What are the benefits of having single, more cohesive policies that blanket entire state rather than different laws in different localities? What are the drawbacks?

Key Concepts

- Dillon's Rule
- Home Rule
- Sovereignty
- Self-governance
- Preemption

For More Information:

https://columbialawreview.org/content/impeding-innovation-state-preemption-of-progressive-local-regulations/

http://www.supportdemocracy.org/2019/07/29/endofsession19/

https://www.cleveland.com/crime/2019/08/dayton-and-all-other-ohio-cities-are-prohibited-by-state-law-from-enacting-gun-control-legislation.html

Works Cited

Catania, S. (2006). *The Importance of Being Ernie*. Mother Jones. https://www.motherjones.com/politics/2006/01/importance-being-ernie/

Mitchell, T. (2017, June 22). *1. The demographics of gun ownership*. Pew Research Center's Social & Demographic Trends Project; Pew Research Center's Social & Demographic Trends Project. https://www.pewsocialtrends.org/2017/06/22/the-demographics-of-gun-ownership/

National Rifle Association. (2018). *Protecting Your Right to Hunt is More Important Than Ever*. NRA-ILA. https://www.nraila.org/articles/20180924/protecting-your-right-to-hunt-is-more-important-than-ever

News 5 Cleveland. (2018, November 1). *Most force incidents involve same Euclid cops*. WEWS. https://www.news5cleveland.com/longform/euclid-officers-named-in-police-brutality-lawsuits-showed-warning-signs-in-use-of-force-reports

Ohio Legislature. (2017). *The Ohio Legislature*. Ohio.Gov. https://www.legislature.ohio.gov/laws/ohio-constitution

Strauss, M. (2018, August 16). *Americans are divided over the use of animals in scientific research*. Pew Research Center; Pew Research Center. https://www.pewresearch.org/fact-tank/2018/08/16/americans-are-divided-over-the-use-of-animals-in-scientific-research/

U.S. Census Bureau. (2019). *U.S. Census Bureau QuickFacts: Euclid city, Ohio*. www.Census.Gov. https://www.census.gov/quickfacts/euclidcityohio

U.S. Fish and Wildlife Services. (2012). *Grizzly bear*. Fws.Gov. https://www.fws.gov/mountain-prairie/es/grizzlyBear.php

Waters, A. (2015). *Austin Resource Recovery Results of the Single-Use Bag Ordinance in Austin, Texas Environmental Effects of the Single Use Bag Ordinance in Austin, Texas*. In Austin Resource Recovery. https://www.austintexas.gov/edims/document.cfm?id=232679

4

BUDGETING, FINANCE, AND FISCAL POLICY

There is a tendency to think of taxes and budgets as dry, technical, and yes, boring. That is a pretty good description of much of the literature on the subject, but a very mistaken view of the subject itself. Actually, budgets are the subject of some of the most intense political struggles in state and local politics. It isn't that people simply care about money (though they do). Budgets are fundamentally about policy. In many ways, they are the central policy documents of governments. They determine and reflect much of the policy orientations of elected leaders. If you want to know what your state or local government's priorities are, its budget will tell you.

One of the areas where state budgeting finance may affect the lives of those reading this the most is as it pertains to the funding of state colleges and universities. In general, the past decade has seen sharp decreases in state funding for higher education. We look closer at the reasons for this and the implications that come along with it. Next, we move on to a discussion of municipal liabilities, specifically liabilities related to paying for pensions and other benefits for public employees. We close this section out back at the state level where we examine the budgeting process and explore why some states have such a hard time passing their budgets.

Tax Cuts and College Tuition, A Louisiana Story

If you started going to a public university in Louisiana in 2008, the state picked up about 60% of the tab. Now, just over a decade later, taxpayers only fund about a quarter of the bill, leaving students and their families to cover the rest in the form of rapidly rising tuition and fees. To take one example, tuition and fees at the University of Louisiana at Lafayette, tuition and fees were less than $3,500 per year in 2008 and are now well over $8,000. In Louisiana this has led to fewer students seeking college degrees. And in a state that has historically lagged in terms of its higher educational attainment (only two states, Arkansas and West Virginia have a smaller percentage of adults with a college degree), this is a big deal (Williams 2018).

While the Louisiana situation is the most severe in the country, they are not alone. The national recession that started in 2008 made it necessary for virtually every state in the union to cut funding for their colleges and universities, and while the economy had, pre-covid, improved considerably from the worst of the recession, funding for public institutions of higher education has not improved in the same way. State funding for public colleges and universities in 2018 was over $7 billion, or about 10%, below 2008 funding levels, even after adjusting for inflation. There are other reasons for the decreased state support for higher education as well. A population that is growing older by the day, aging infra-structure, and inflation have all lead to tighter budgets and a continuing push to lower taxes has left states with less money to dole out (Mitchell, Leachman, and Masterson 2017).

In response, colleges have taken measures like reducing faculty, decreasing pay raises for faculty and staff, limiting course offerings, shuttering small majors and programs, and even closing satellite campuses in some cases. The main response to the drastic decrease in state funding for these schools, however, has been to increase tuition. And oh how it has increased. In 2017-18, for the first time ever, tuition revenue was more than the government appropriation in for public institutions of higher education in the majority of the states. In Delaware, New Hampshire, and Vermont, more than 70% of the funding for higher educa-tion came from tuition dollars. All in all, tuition revenue per student increased in 33 states and has risen 36% over the past decade and by a whopping 96% in the past 25 years. Across the country, the average price of tuition, fees, and room and board is over $20,000 (Seltzer 2018a).

During his 2016 presidential run, Bernie Sanders called for free tuition for the nation's public colleges and universities, arguing that there is a precedent: "Making public colleges and universities tuition-free, that exists in countries all over the world, used to exist in the United States." (Sanders 2016). He wasn't wrong either. Countries like Denmark, Estonia, Finland, Germany, Norway, Slovak Republic, Slovenia, Sweden, and Turkey all offer tuition-free public edu-cation. The state picks up the tab. And, indeed, there are many schools in the U.S. that used to be tuition-free. California, for example, did not charge tuition to in-state students until the 1970s.

Some argue that it should be the responsibility of the student and their family to pay for college. Why should the taxpayer be on the hook for someone else's education? Well, there is an answer to that. Increased tuition decreases students' access to education and increases the debt load of student coming out of school. This holds true in particular for low-income students, students of color, and non-traditional students. This matters to all of us, whether we choose to go to college or not. On average, someone with a college degree will earn almost a million dollars more than a comparable high school graduate over the course of their working life (Carnevale, Rose, and Cheah 2018). That's $900,000 that can be spent on things. We like it when people spend money on things. That's what we are talking about when we talk about THE ECONOMY (plus a couple other things like production and imports/exports, but those things are better too when people have money to spend). Say you're a high school graduate who takes over the family landscaping business after graduation. Landscaping can be a prosperous line of work. You know what makes it more prosperous? Customers. Customers who can afford the luxury of hiring out their lawn care. This works for pretty much any business you can think of. We all do better when we are all doing better, and college degrees generally up our earning capacity. Does this mean that there is no value in the jobs and trades that don't require a college degree? Of course not. Re-read this paragraph. We all do better when we all do better. If Joe CollegeGrad gets an awesome job as an accountant and starts earning tons of money, maybe he will build a new house to hold all of his shiny new things. He will need a contractor, and that contractor will hire framers, drywallers, plumbers, electricians, painters, roofers … and probably even landscapers. Joe needs those people to build his house. Those people need Joe's business. Maybe they will even turn around and hire him to do their accounting.

Increased college costs have a particularly harsh impact on students of color. A 2019 Study by Drew Allen and Gregory Wolniak found that at non-selective schools, a $1000 increase in tuition costs lead to a 4.5% drop in diversity in freshman classes (Seltzer 2018b). In Louisiana, the historically black universities have seen a precipitous drop in enrollment, 15% in the last decade (March 2016). People who had been left behind in the past are the first to be left behind once again. And while student loan debt is a burden on many—according to the National Center for Education statistics, over 44 million Americans owe over $1.48 trillion in student loan debt (National Center for Education Statistics 2017)—again, this is even worse for people of color. According to a recent study done by Jason Houle and Fenaba Addo, black students take on 85% more student loan debt than their white counterparts. Then, because black families have, on average, less household income and net wealth than white families, it takes longer for black students to pay back their loans. The researchers found that white borrowers pay their student debt down at about 10% per year, while black borrowers only pay down 4% per year. This means that after fifteen years the black borrower owes 185% more loan debt than the white borrower (Addo, Houle, and Simon 2016).

This is a problem for multiple reasons. First, we can talk again about the economic impact of having significant debt. Each penny that goes toward a student loan payment is a penny that doesn't go toward building a house. Or buying anything. No business for the landscaper. Remember, we want people to buy things. Capitalism requires money circulating around.

There is a moral issue at play here too. Along with policies such as slavery, institutionalized and de facto job discrimination, housing discrimination, and a host of other things, that America's colleges and universities have historically denied the privilege of higher education to people of color have combined to systematically deprive some Americans access to much of the wealth that has accumulated over time. Public universities have been thought to be an opportunity for many to "pull themselves up by the bootstraps" and become more financially successful than the generations before, but if your parents aren't able to help pay your tuition, and the tuition is too high to pay as you go, high student loan debt or simply not attending might be the only options. In other words, the disadvantages faced in the past are leading to disadvantages now and in the future.

America's public colleges and universities used to stand as a beacon to young people. Work hard, get good grades, go to college, and you will be able to move up in the world. In the modern climate of undervaluing higher education and overvaluing tax cuts, that beacon isn't shining quite as brightly.

Discussion Questions

1. Should maintaining a public university system be the taxpayers' responsibility? Why or why not?
2. What benefits does a public university bring to a community? To a state?
3. What would happen if all universities were private?
4. Should the federal government charge interest on student loans? Why or why not?

Key Concepts

- Recession
- Economy
- Inflation
- Capitalism

For More Information:

https://www.washingtonpost.com/education/2018/09/08/states-decision-reduce-support-higher-education-comes-cost/?noredirect=on&utm_term=.1bc0a1e11c9a

https://www.pewtrusts.org/en/research-and-analysis/blogs/stateline/2018/
03/29/tuition-overtakes-state-money-as-funding-source-for-public-colleges
https://link.springer.com/article/10.1007%2Fs11162-018-9502-6
https://thirdway.imgix.net/pdfs/override/IsCollegeWorthIt-FINAL.pdf
https://hechingerreport.org/the-devastating-impact-in-the-state-thats-cut-
higher-education-the-most/

Is Grandpa Bankrupting Your City?
A Look at Debts and Liabilities

If you pay any attention at all to the national news, it won't surprise you to
know that the national debt is staggering. It is also increasing rapidly; it hit
$22 trillion for the first time in February of 2019 (Trimble 2019). What you
might not have heard about is the $2 trillion in debt that is owed locally. How,
you might be wondering, is that even possible? Don't states and localities (save
for Vermont) have to balance their budgets? Are they even allowed to borrow
money?

Well, you are right to wonder these things. Most municipal debt does not
come from borrowing money to cover gaps between expenditures and revenue.
Most of it stems from the unfunded liabilities piling up from public pension
plans. We call these legacy costs—expenses that were incurred in the past but
have to be paid for now. If your grandfather was a city employee, for instance,
and had a retirement plan that guaranteed him a certain number of dollars per
month after he retired, that is a deal—a contract that the city made with ol'
gramps. But it means that they have to keep paying that to him, and all of the
other people who retired from the city with the same retirement plans, for the
rest of their lives.

This would be okay as long as the city planned appropriately for paying these
expenses. The account that they pay the pensions from has to be properly funded,
and if the money is invested, cities need to be realistic about what kind of returns
they can reasonably expect when they invest the money. Unfortunately, this has
not been the case in many municipalities. Pressure to keep cutting taxes and an
overly-optimistic reliance on investment income has created some pretty serious problems for city leaders. And, as legacy costs continue to go up, cities end
up with less and less money to pay for the things we expect—police, fire, road
repairs, snow removal, and other critical services.

Milwaukee is a particularly good (bad?) example of this legacy problem.
Between 2006 and 2016 Milwaukee's debt grew by almost 41% and they are
spending more than a third of their budget on debt service. And then if you add
in the contributions that they make to the account for future pension expenses,
they spend over 43% of their budget just on these items. This is the highest share
of spending of any city over 500,000 in the country (Maciag, 2017).

Perhaps it isn't that much of a surprise, seeing rust-belt cities face debt problems. We know that cities like Detroit, Scranton, and yes, Milwaukee, have faced a decline in the manufacturing industries that had been their bread and butter for decades. When businesses shutter and the population stop increasing, it is difficult for cities to manage continuing to pay for benefits for city employees that had been earned while the city was thriving. But what about a city that has one of the fastest growing economies in the country? One with hundreds of multinational companies, a growing population, and a big-money CEO as its mayor? This might not be the city you would expect to have debt problems stemming from legacy costs, but you'd be wrong. In late 2016 and early 2017, Dallas, Texas almost went bankrupt.

In the past, Dallas city officials offered solid pension plans to the city's police officers and fire fighters. One of the benefits of these plans was the ability to withdraw cash from the plan in large chunks. In 2016, rumors started flying that the city was facing financial uncertainty based on some risky investments that they had made and that officials were considering changing the pension policy and no longer allowing retirees to withdraw blocks of money. The retirees freaked out at this news and ran to withdraw money while they still could. They pulled $220 million out of the pension fund in only six weeks. In order to restock the fund and get it up to a reasonable, but not fully funded, size, the trustees of the fund asked for an infusion of over $1 billion, which is the equivalent to an entire year's general fund budget for the whole city, but didn't even come close to the $7 billion that the pension fund was in debt. Basically, if Dallas were to fix the pension fund problem, they would not be able to pay for, literally, anything else for the year. This was not possible (Walsh 2016).

Luckily for the citizens of Dallas, city leadership, along with the state legislature and Governor, was able to patch together a solution to stabilize the pension fund. Unfortunately for the city's firefighters and police officers, this meant a reduction in future benefits and an increase in employee contributions. The retirement age was raised, cost of living increases was decreased, and the rule that allowed retirees to withdraw chunks of money was eliminated. These changes have slowed the leaking certainly, however the fund will have to be re-examined seven years after the new rules took effect (Walsh 2016).

This tinkering with the benefits worked in Texas but wouldn't have helped in some other states. This is because most states follow what is known as a "contract rights" approach to pension benefits. California is a big leader in this regard. In 1955, there was a case called Allen v. City of Long Beach (Allen v City of Long Beach 1955). The ruling held that workers are essentially entering into a contract with their employers when they start the job and that the pension and other benefits that are offered are part of that contract, and thus cannot be unilaterally decreased. There are twelve other states that follow the so-called "California Rule" and a bunch of others that have adopted a similar approach.

The California Rule has recently come under scrutiny though as a case, Cal Fire Local 2881 v. CalPERS (when you see the letters PERS, they refer to the public employee retirement system, so IPERS is the Iowa Public Employee Retirement System, for instance). In California, the public employees were offered the opportunity to purchase additional retirement services as part of their benefits package. In 2013, though, the state eliminated this decade-old benefit and under the auspices of the California Rule, one of the firefighter unions sued. The question at hand was whether the firefighters had a contractual right to that particular benefit (League of California Cities n.d.).

While the California Supreme Court could have taken this opportunity to address the entirety of the California Rule, they declined to do so. Thus, the California Rule is still intact—mostly. They did rule that the opportunity to purchase additional retirement services was not part of the core benefits package and that by offering this additional service temporarily the California legislature did not intend to create a contractual obligation. This may change in the near future as there are three more upcoming cases addressing similar issues: Marin Association of Public Employees v. Marin County Employees' Retirement Association, Alameda Deputy Sheriff's Association v. Alameda County Employees' Retirement Association, and Hipsher v. Los Angeles County Retirement Association.

There is a real tension between delivering on the promises that were made in the past to the nation's public employees and the realities of financing these benefits. As more and more cities, counties, and even states are seeing the results of over-promising benefits to public workers and underfunding accounts, there are really only three options: decrease benefits (where and if that is a possibility), increase taxes (not so popular with voters), or take money from other programs to pay for the benefits (also not very popular with voters). As they say, something has got to give.

Discussion Questions

1. How does the pressure to cut taxes fit in with this section?
2. What is the difference between a pension and a retirement account? What are the pros and cons of each?
3. Do you agree with the State of California that workers are essentially in a contract with their employer? Why or why not? What are the implications?
4. Even when many public employees are seeing jobs and benefits cut, police and firefighters are more likely to maintain their status quo. What might be some reasons for this?

Key Concepts

- National Debt
- Unfunded liability

- Pension
- Legacy costs
- Contract rights
- California Rule
- Public Employee Retirement System

For More Information:

https://wispolicyforum.org/focus/is-municipal-debt-rising-too-fast/
https://www.usnews.com/opinion/economic-intelligence/articles/2017-01-03/how-cities-get-into-fiscal-trouble
https://www.nytimes.com/2017/06/01/business/dealbook/municipal-pensions-dallas-houston-bankruptcy.html
https://thehill.com/blogs/pundits-blog/economy-budget/324125-worried-about-the-national-debt-its-even-worse-for-our
http://www.governing.com/topics/finance/gov-legacy-cities-bills-debt.html
https://www.nytimes.com/2016/11/21/business/dealbook/dallas-pension-debt-threat-of-bankruptcy.html

Isn't That Their Job? How State Legislatures End Up Not Passing Budgets

In July 2017, the New Jersey Star-Ledger published pictures of then-Governor Chris Christie and his family lounging on a beach at Island Beach State Park (Mills and Brodesser-Akner 2017), soaking up the rays without any noisy crowds to bother them. What could have been pictures of any American family enjoying a quiet day by the water came with loads of criticism though. The problem was that due to a budget impasse and the resulting shutdown of the New Jersey government, all of the state beaches were closed.

Like many states, New Jersey has a July 1 deadline to pass a budget. When July 1, 2017 came and went with no agreed-upon budget, Governor Christie signed an executive order that immediately shutdown non-essential government functions during what is typically an extremely busy holiday weekend. The shutdown only lasted three days, but the impacts were felt by both the citizens of New Jersey who didn't have access to many government services during that time, and by the businesses surrounding the shuttered beaches that rely on busy holidays to make money (Corasaniti 2017).

Christie's beachy exploits earned New Jersey some national media, but there were actually eleven states that started fiscal year 2018 without budgets (and another ten that only passed them by calling special sessions of legislature) and since 2002, 19 states have started at least one fiscal year without a finalized budget. Five of these states ended up with a partial government shutdown as a result (Farmer 2017). To be sure, some of the states have plans in place to continue operations without a budget, but many do not, leading to serious threats to the continuation of government operations and major financial implications. Calling special legislative sessions or holding the legislature longer than usual increases operating costs. Sending state employees home, known as furloughing, also has costs. In Pennsylvania's 2008 shutdown, it was estimated that $3.5 million in wages were lost (Urbina 2007). No income taxes are collected from those employees during the furlough, so that is lost money for the government. And then those employees don't have money to go spend, which hurts the economy even further.

There are three major reasons that states are sometimes unable to pass their budgets on time: the fiscal conditions in the state, partisan politics, and the individual states' rules and procedures regarding budgeting.

The nationwide recession in the 2000s caused significant budget shortfalls pretty much everywhere. Trying to decide what to find and what gets cut when there simply isn't as much money as there used to be understandably led to complicated budget negations during this time period. Think of it this way—the state collects tax money from income, sales, and property taxes (not all states use all of these, but the point remains the same). During the recession, fewer people were working, so they weren't paying as much in income taxes. People who aren't working or who lost money in real estate or the stock market don't buy as many things, so the amount of sales taxes the states bring in drops. And when the housing market crashed, property tax revenue crashed right along with it. In fiscal year 2010, states faced a cumulative budget gap of over $145 billion. Nine states (Arizona, California, Connecticut, Illinois, Michigan, Mississippi, North Carolina, Ohio, and Pennsylvania) began the year without a finalized budget (National Conference of State Legislatures 2010).

It should come as no surprise that partisan politics also leads to squabbles that can cause a late budget. We saw an example of this in the Pacific Northwest in 2017. In 2016, a Supreme Court decision on private water wells ended up preventing many rural landowners from digging new wells (Sokol 2016). The Republicans in Washington State took this up as a major issue, insisting that a fix for this problem should be the highest priority for the state. In fact, they said, it was so important that they were willing to hold up the entire capital spending budget for the year in order to get a bill passed. They could do it, too. Washington requires a 60% majority to approve capital spending and the Republicans were numerous enough that the budget couldn't be passed without them. Partisan maneuvering held up the capital spending budget through the entire season.

States set up their own rules and procedures for how their budgets get deliberated on and enacted and there is quite a bit of variation involved. For instance, there are a few states that require a supermajority to vote to pass a budget appropriation bill (generally either two-thirds or three-fifths of the votes). The idea is that the budget should be more reasonable in terms of where the money is going if more people have to agree on it. There is mixed evidence for the effectiveness of this tactic though, as some have found that states actually end up spending MORE money in order to put together a large enough coalition of lawmakers to pass the budget. If you and 99 of your closest friends are going to order food from Alfredo's Pizza Cafe and 66 of you have to agree on the order before you can place it, you may end up ordering more food than you would if only 51 of you needed to agree on the order because you are adding fifteen more opinions and food preferences into the mix. Thus, rules about how budgets get passed can lead to delays and late budgets.

As the new fiscal year gets underway here, we are seeing a far different picture than only a couple of years ago. There are two key reasons for this. First, there is less political gridlock than there was before. A state government trifecta is when a single political party holds the governorship and majority control of both houses of the legislature. After the 2018 elections, 36 states have a trifecta, fourteen controlled by Democrats and 22 by Republicans (State government trifectas, 2020). Does having a single party in control of government mean that there won't be squabbling over the budget? Heck no! Ask New Jersey or Illinois about that. It is true though that one-party states tend to have less political gridlock and that makes it easier to pass budgets on time.

The bigger difference for most states though is a fiscal one. The United States is in a better place financially that it has been for a while. Unemployment is low and the stock market is doing well. A couple of states have raised taxes on the highest income earners. Additionally, many states have started collecting sales taxes from online sales after a 2018 Supreme Court ruling changed the old rule that had prevented them from doing so. According to the National Association of State Budget Officers (NASBO), there are at least 28 states that have exceeded their projections for how much revenue they expected to bring in during 2019 and almost all of the states, 47 of them, are planning on increasing spending in the 2020 fiscal year (National Association of State Budget Officers 2020).

Unsurprisingly, it is easier for state governments to agree on spending money when there is money to spend, and there are a couple different areas that are benefitting from the influx of tax money. Many states are increasing their education spending. In fact, NASBO reports that almost 2/3 of new spending in the states is being used on education. For example, Minnesota is directing an increase of $718 million toward K-12 education and another $165 for higher education. Considering the spending cuts in education, especially in higher education, that increased drastically in the wake of the Great Recession, increases such as those in Minnesota are welcomed by education officials (National Association of State Budget Officers 2020).

During the Great Recession, states had also cut money from transportation and infrastructure funding. These areas are also seeing increased funding for fiscal year 2020. Four states, Alabama, Arkansas, Illinois, and Ohio raised their gas taxes and according to the American Road and Transportation Builders Association, lawmakers in 37 states had introduced 185 bills in the first couple of months of 2019 alone designed to increase investment in transportation and infrastructure (National Conference of State Legislators 2020). This is particularly important, as many people are concerned about the condition of America's roads and other infrastructure (The American Society of Civil Engineers assigns the U.S. infrastructure a report card–like grade each year, and we are currently sitting at an average of D+, so ... not great) (American Society of Civil Engineers 2017).

When states don't pass their budgets, there can be consequences. Sure, there are stopgap measures, like continuing resolutions or temporary appropriation bills and twelve states have provisions that allow for payment to agencies and for services even if a budget isn't passed, but in 22 states if a budget isn't passed, the government shuts down. Employees are furloughed and sent home. Parks are closed, services are put on hiatus. Not only does this cost a ton of money (see above), but there are also long-term effects in terms of damage to the state's image and to the public's confidence in their government.

Discussion Questions

1. If a state is having financial trouble (like in the wake of the recession), what are some reasons that the leadership might still cut taxes?
2. To what extent should a governor have to suffer along with their citizens during a shutdown by not using facilities that are closed to the public?
3. If a legislature feels very strongly about a topic, how should they balance using the potential to hold up the budget to get what they want with the potential negative outcomes that come with a shutdown?
4. During times where states' finances are good, should they have to put aside money for the future or do they have a responsibility to give the money back to the citizens?
5. What do you consider to be essential services that would have to stay open during a shutdown?

Key Concepts

- Budget
- Executive order
- Government shutdown
- Fiscal year

- Furlough
- Recession
- Budget shortfall

For More Information:

https://www.nasbo.org/reports-data/fiscal-survey-of-states
https://www.governing.com/week-in-finance/gov-supreme-court-clears-tax-internet-sales.html
https://www.cbpp.org/research/state-budget-and-tax/a-lost-decade-in-higher-education-funding

Works Cited

Addo, F. R., Houle, J. N., & Simon, D. (2016). Young, Black, and (Still) in the Red: Parental Wealth, Race, and Student Loan Debt. *Race and Social Problems*, 8(1), 64–76. https://www.ncbi.nlm.nih.gov/pmc/articles/PMC6049093/

American Society of Civil Engineers. (2017). *ASCE's 2017 American Infrastructure Report Card*. Infrastructure Report Card. https://www.infrastructurereportcard.org

Ballotpedia. (2020, October 12). *State government trifectas*. https://ballotpedia.org/State_government_trifectas

Carnevale, A., Rose, S., & Cheah, B. (2018, October 25). *The College Payoff*. CEW Georgetown. https://cew.georgetown.edu/cew-reports/the-college-payoff/

Corasaniti, N. (2017, June 30). New Jersey Government Shuts Down Over Budget Standoff (Published 2017). *The New York Times*. https://www.nytimes.com/2017/06/30/nyregion/chris-christie-new-jersey-budget.html

Farmer, L. (2017). *As Political Division Grows, State Budgets Come in Later (If at All)*. Www.Governing.Com. https://www.governing.com/topics/finance/gov-record-number-late-state-budgets-this-year.html

League of California Cities. (n.d.). *The California Supreme Court's Ruling*. Retrieved October 12, 2020, from https://www.cacities.org/Resources-Documents/Policy-Advocacy-Section/Hot-Issues/Pension-Resources/LCC-Supreme-Court-ver2.aspx

Maciag, M. (2017). City Debt Spending Continues to Rise. Government Technology. https://www.govtech.com/fs/infrastructure/City-Debt-Spending-Continues-to-Rise.html

March, S. (2016). *Negative race relations spark HBCU enrollment increase*. The Times. https://www.shreveporttimes.com/story/news/education/2016/06/29/louisianas-historically-black-colleges-seeing-modest-enrollment-increase/85699670/

Mills, A., & Brodesser-Akner, C. (2017, July 3). *Christie, family soak up sun on beach he closed*. Nj. https://www.nj.com/politics/2017/07/christie_pictured_at_island_beach_state_park_durin.html

Mitchell, M., Leachman, M., & Masterson, K. (2017, October 11). *A Lost Decade in Higher Education Funding*. Center on Budget and Policy Priorities. https://www.cbpp.org/research/state-budget-and-tax/a-lost-decade-in-higher-education-funding

National Association of State Budget Officers. (2020). *Fiscal Survey of the States - Nasbo*. Www.Nasbo.Org. https://www.nasbo.org/reports-data/fiscal-survey-of-states

National Center for Education Statistics. (2017). *The NCES Fast Facts Tool provides quick answers to many education questions (National Center for Education Statistics)*. Nces.Ed.Gov. https://nces.ed.gov/fastfacts/display.asp?id=900

National Conference of State Legislatures. (2010). *Late State Budgets*. https://www.ncsl.org/research/fiscal-policy/late-state-budgets.aspx

National Conference of State Legislatures. (2020). *Recent Legislative Actions Likely to Change Gas Taxes*. https://www.ncsl.org/research/transportation/2013-and-2014-legislative-actions-likely-to-change-gas-taxes.aspx

Sanders, B. (2016, February 5). Transcript of the Democratic Presidential Debate (Published 2016). *The New York Times*. https://www.nytimes.com/2016/02/05/us/politics/transcript-of-the-democratic-presidential-debate.html

Seltzer, R. (2018a). *State support for higher ed increased in 2017, but so did tuition revenue.* Www.Insidehighered.Com. https://www.insidehighered.com/news/2018/03/29/state-support-higher-ed-increased-2017-so-did-tuition-revenue

Seltzer, R. (2018b). *Tuition Hikes Hurt Diversity*. Inside Higher Ed. https://www.insidehighered.com/news/2018/03/27/increases-college-tuition-drive-down-diversity-public-colleges-study-says

Sokol, C. (2016). *Washington Supreme Court water-rights ruling will affect building permits for rural property owners | The Spokesman-Review*.Www.Spokesman.Com. https://www.spokesman.com/stories/2016/oct/18/washington-supreme-court-water-rights-ruling-will-/

Trimble, M. (2019). *National Debt Tops $22 Trillion for First Time*. US News & World Report; U.S. News & World Report. https://www.usnews.com/news/national-news/articles/2019-02-13/national-debt-surpasses-22-trillion-for-first-time-in-history

Urbina, I. (2007, July 9). Government Shutdown in Pennsylvania. *The New York Times*. https://www.nytimes.com/2007/07/09/us/09cnd-penn.html

Walsh, M.W. (2016, November 20). Dallas Stares Down a Texas-Size Threat of Bankruptcy (Published 2016). *The New York Times*. https://www.nytimes.com/2016/11/21/business/dealbook/dallas-pension-debt-threat-of-bankruptcy.html

Williams, C. J. (2018). *Since 2008, fees at UL Lafayette have almost tripled, causing concerns for students, professors*. The Vermilion. https://www.thevermilion.com/news/since-2008-fees-at-ul-lafayette-have-almost-tripled-causing-concerns-for-students-professors/article_02d4c87a-e16f-11e8-b7ae-03490d93c13e.html

5

ELECTIONS AND POLITICAL PARTICIPATION

There is a weird phenomenon here in the U.S. We hold more elections than any other country on earth, yet we show up to vote at them at lower rates than pretty much anyone else. Elections may be how citizens can speak out for their beliefs and they may give states a voice in national politics, but you wouldn't know it from the interest they generate among the general public.

This chapter looks at both electoral participation and other kinds of participation as well. We start by considering an academic study where the researchers use peer pressure to try to increase voter turnout. Spoiler alert: people are more likely to go vote if they think their friends and neighbors are doing a better job of being civically engaged than they are. In the second part, we move on to talk about election security. In the past couple of elections, it has become increasingly clear that there may be some cause for concern in this area, however there is some disagreement about this. Finally, we look at another academic article that considers the internet as a tool for increasing political participation.

Social Pressure and Voter Turnout

As the German philosopher Hegel once noted, "The casting of a single vote is of no significance where there is a multitude of electors" (Hegel 1991, p. 203). This is the *instrumental* view of voting. The chance that your vote will determine the outcome of an election is so very tiny that we might wonder why people choose to vote at all. After all, while we often dwell on the fact that voter turnout in the U.S. is relatively low compared to other industrialized countries (and compared to itself in previous decades), millions of people turn out to vote each year in various federal, state, local, and special elections.

One group of researchers decided to look deeper into the factors that cause people to show up at the polls. Alan Gerber, Donald Green, and Christopher Larimer (Gerber, Green, and Larimer 2008) noted that there are two types of motivation for voting: intrinsic and extrinsic. Intrinsic motivation involves engaging in a behavior because it is rewarding in itself to the person engaging in that behavior. They are doing that thing for its own sake instead of for the promise or threat of a reward or punishment. On the other hand, extrinsic motivation is when something external is motivating us, through rewards or punishments, to do something. You do the thing, not because you want to, necessarily, but because you want the reward or to avoid the punishment. Think of it this way, you may know people who run for exercise. Heck, you may be one of those people. Some people run because they love it. They enjoy the feeling that it gives them and the opportunity to go out and have some solitary time, or listen to music, or whatever. Other people run because they feel an external pressure to exercise. Everyone in their social group might be doing it. They might want to be perceived as an athletic person. That first person has intrinsic motivation, running for the sake of running. The second person has external motivation, running for the "reward" of being part of a group or being seen in a certain way.

Gerber, Green, and Larimer posit that this same system might be working for voting, and furthermore that certain types of extrinsic pressures are highly effective in terms of getting people to get out and vote. Some people (certainly not the majority) just like voting. It makes them feel good, like they are performing their civic duty and like they are part of something bigger than themselves. People like this feel intrinsically rewarded by voting. They participate in the system for its own sake. But what about the people who need more extrinsic motivation to vote? After all, in the U.S. we don't really reward or punish people for voting or not (and some places do … see Australia for an example of a country with compulsory voting and punishments for failing to participate).

One interesting thing about Americans is that we lie about whether we voted or not. When pollsters ask people whether they voted in the last election, most of them will say yes, of course they voted. But when you compare these numbers to the actual turnout data, it becomes obvious that not nearly so many people had voted in reality. The fact that this occurs over and over indicates a social desirability bias with regard to voting. People answer the question in a way that they think will be viewed favorably by others rather than answering truthfully.

Although this phenomenon is frustrating for pollsters and others trying to make predictions about election results, there is also an opportunity for researchers to better understand how to increase voter turnout. And this is where Gerber, Green, and Larimer come back in. They got the list of all 180,002 households appearing in the "Qualified Voter File" state voter list in Michigan for the 2006 election. They split the sample up into 5 groups, a control group (one that they won't do anything to, in order to compare the other groups to it) and then four different mailings.

The first group was mailed a postcard that appealed to the individual's sense of civic duty. The card literally said "DO YOUR CIVIC DUTY—VOTE!", and "Remember your rights and responsibilities as a citizen. Remember to vote" (Gerber, Green, and Larimer 2008, p. 37). The second group received a mailing that included the reference to civic duty but added a light social pressure, telling the voter they are being studied by researchers and that whether they voted was a matter of public record. The purpose here is along the lines of the Hawthorne effect[1], testing whether observation would make a difference for turnout. The next group's mailing took the pressure a step further, reminding the recipients that their voting history was a matter of public record and listing the recent voting records of the members of the household. This was designed to test whether the pressure of the other members of the household knowing whether they voted or not would influence turnout. The last group got the most pressure. Their mailing listed the household voting records from the last election AND the records of their neighbors. The card let the recipients know that they intended to send an updated mailer after the election to let them know who voted and who did not. This was designed to exert maximum social pressure on the recipients.

Voter records are generally publicly available. Not WHO you voted for, but often what party you are registered with and whether you voted or not in any given election. The researchers got these records after the 2006 election was over to see whether their experiment had impacted turnout. Their results were pretty clear. The group that hadn't received any mailings, the control group, had a turnout rate of 29.7%. The group that had gotten the card reminding them of their civic duty turned out a little more frequently at a rate of 31.5%. The group that was told they were being observed by researchers had slightly better numbers, with a 32.2% turnout rate. So, these little nudges did make a difference, albeit a small one.

The groups who got the social pressure mailings had even higher turnout compared to the control group. When the researchers sent the recipients their household voting records, their turnout increased to 34.5% and when the neighborhood voting records were included turnout jumped way up to 37.8%, an 8.1% increase. This is a bigger effect than any of the experiments that had come before it, like looking at the effect of meeting a candidate face-to-face or receiving live reminder phone calls or even having same-day voter registration.

During the 2014 election, an app was introduced in Oregon called, "didtheyvote.org" where you could log on and type in your friends' names and find out if they voted. Other similar apps, like VoteWithMe and OutVote followed. These programs are simply pulling information that is already public and repackaging it for easy consumption, allowing you to pretty easily sleuth the voting habits of, well, pretty much anyone you want. Again, no one can see who you voted for, just your party affiliation and whether or not you voted at all, but the idea is based on the same implications as the Gerber, Green, and Larimer study. People vote in higher numbers if they think they are being observed. These apps are pretty much just automating that same process.

Discussion Questions

1. Why do people often lie when they are asked if they voted in the last election? What does that tell us about intrinsic versus extrinsic motivation to vote?
2. It is ethical to pressure people into voting? Explain.
3. Did you know that voter records are generally publicly available? What are the pros and cons of this?
4. Do you think that you, personally, are more intrinsically or extrinsically motivated when it comes to voting? What makes you think this?

Key Concepts

- Voter turnout
- Intrinsic motivation
- Extrinsic motivation
- Compulsory voting
- Social pressure

For More Information

https://isps.yale.edu/sites/default/files/publication/2012/12/ISPS08-001.pdf
https://www.sciencedirect.com/science/article/pii/S0261379415300032
https://www.9news.com/article/news/local/next/whats-with-the-voting-report-card-sent-to-colorado-voters/73-2e90961e-76cc-4fdd-ae5c-f0dfafb238e3
https://thomasleeper.com/2014/10/montana-experiment/

Cybersecurity and Election Systems: When Is It Time to Panic?

In July of 2016, the U.S. Office of Cybersecurity and Communications at the Department of Homeland Security made a disturbing discovery. Someone had hacked the Illinois Board of Elections. The intruders had quietly infiltrated the election system and spent weeks poking around. They ultimately found the state's voter-registration database and were able to download the registration information on hundreds of thousands of Illinois voters. The following month they learned that it had happened again, this time in Arizona. The hackers stole information from the voter-registration database and installed malware into the system (Department of Homeland Security 2016).

It was agents of the federal government that initially made these discoveries, but the federal government does not control elections in the U.S. In fact, when DHS decided it was time to contact the officials that actually run elections, they encountered a problem. There are more than 10,000 electoral jurisdictions in the United States, and in August of 2016, we were only weeks away from the start of early voting for the 2016 midterm elections.

The U.S. has a decentralized election system. The entities that do the nitty gritty tasks of actually running an election are typically at the local level—counties and municipalities. The state is responsible for a few aspects of elections, and the federal government plays a very small role as well. Ultimately, states all differ in how they run their elections, and there is even quite a bit of variation in how elections work within the states.

Over the years, as elections grew bigger and more complex, many election authorities have moved to electronic forms of voting and/or tabulation. The swing toward electronic forms of voting accelerated after the debacle that was the 2000 election in Florida (if you have never heard the terms "butterfly ballot" or "hanging chad", consider yourself lucky). It seemed like electronic voting was the way to go.

There are several different versions of balloting that are assisted by electronics. There are voting machines that are entirely electronic—you choose your preferred candidate right there on the screen and the machine keeps track of who you voted for. On some of these machines, a paper copy is printed for you to check the accuracy of the vote that was recorded for you and for officials to use to check against the electronic count. Five states are completely paperless though, relying on the machines to keep an accurate count themselves. Other states use paper ballots that are then scanned into a computer that does the tallying. Again, then you have the paper copies to check to make sure the count is correct if you need to (Good 2018).

According to intelligence experts, the electronic nature of the machines is risky. Some state officials argue that the electronic voting machines are secure and that they are never connected to the internet or to each other so they can't be hacked. Experts aren't so sure. They point out that the machines are programmed at some point before the election and that system infiltration could happen then. In fact, one of the companies that makes and maintains voting machines did have a security breach prior to the 2018 election (though there is no evidence that any serious malfeasance happened before the breach was caught). Further, they note, when the results from each individual machine are brought in to tally up the totals, the computers and systems that are used for that process could be vulnerable (Schwartz 2018).

Ensuring the security of these systems takes time and manpower and equipment. Time and manpower and equipment are not cheap. It is estimated that 35% of all of the voting machines used across the U.S. in 2018 were at least ten years old. A federal judge found that Georgia's voting equipment is so old and flawed and vulnerable to failure or breach that she told them that they have to stop using it after 2019. Replacing all of these systems and upgrading the security on the newer systems costs money. In March of 2018, Congress allocated

$380 million for state and local election security. Many states were able to upgrade their equipment to newer, more secure voting machines. For example, Arkansas was able to provide new equipment to 54 of its 75 counties, meaning that over two-thirds of Arkansas voters will be able to vote more securely than before. Many other state and local election officials have said that the allocation wasn't enough. And this is on top of former Special Counsel Robert Mueller's warning that election interference was a problem in 2016 and is likely to be at least as bad in 2020.

Some members of Congress have introduced new bills designed to increase election security. One includes more than $1 billion in funding for state and local governments to improve their security. One requires that vendors of voting equipment be federally certified in the security protocols. Still, another would increase communication between federal intelligence agencies and state/local election officials. These proposals, even though many of them are bipartisan, have been thwarted in the Senate. Mitch McConnell, the Senate Majority Leader, has no interest in allowing these bills to cross from his desk to the chamber to be voted on. His perspective is that the federal government is doing enough. They sanctioned Russia for the last round of hacking. They spent $380 million. Heck, the 2018 midterm election happened with no major incidents.

He isn't wrong. There are zero cases of suspected hacking where vote results were tampered with. Zero cases where hackers caused someone's vote to be recorded differently than they had entered it. While the latter has certainly happened, those cases have been found to be the result of equipment malfunction rather than bad actors. Their overriding message is that we need to remain vigilant about election security so that we can pay more attention to what is on the ballot rather than the ballot itself.

Discussion Questions

1. To what extent should the federal government take over some more aspects of elections because of the risk of outside interference?
2. In regard to the above, could they even do that if they wanted to? Is there anything in the U.S. Constitution that would allow them to do that?
3. What are the benefits of using electronic ballots? Who are the stakeholders here and why does it matter?

Key Concepts

- Boards of Elections
- Decentralization
- Cybersecurity

For More Information:

http://www.ncsl.org/research/elections-and-campaigns/election-administration-at-state-and-local-levels.aspx
https://fas.org/sgp/crs/misc/R45549.pdf
https://www.nytimes.com/2019/06/07/us/politics/election-security-mitch-mcconnell.html

Is the Internet a Tool or a Distraction for Increasing Political Participation?

Political participation is the voluntary engagement in the activities by which leaders are chosen and policy is made. Voting is the most obvious (and the most common) form of active participation, but there are many others. Discussing politics, attending party meetings or campaign rallies, donating money to a campaign or party, or simply communicating with your representatives are all forms of political participation.

It has been said that political participation is a cornerstone of representative democracy. After all, how can an elected official actually represent us if they don't know our preferences? And those elected officials are going to be making decisions about how to spend our tax money and how to organize our society whether you participate or not. "But, in the United States, the choice to not participate is just that, a CHOICE", you might say. And you are right. There are countries that have mandatory voting, and heck, there are countries where there is no chance for political participation at all. The freedom to go to a rally for Alexandria Ocasio-Cortez or for Donald Trump or to stay home and watch Rick and Morty is way up there in terms of things that we value about our system of government in the U.S.

Who decides to engage with the political system matters though. This is of particular interest to those who run campaigns, of course, but also to social scientists. People who fail to participate, whether out of apathy, disenfranchisement, anger, bitterness, or life circumstances, end up wielding less power than those who do participate. This becomes particularly interesting/disturbing when you look at the patterns. We know from research that some groups of people are less likely to engage politically than others. For instance, young people (at least historically), people of color, people with lower incomes, those with less education, and disabled people are all less likely to vote or attend rallies or contact their representatives.

Dating all the way back to Aristotle, philosophers have lauded political participation as a means of using crowdsourcing to do better. Involving as many people as possible should, according to such minds as John Dewey and the author typing this, propose stability, foster creative problem-solving, and prevent tyranny. We all have talents and knowledge and experiences. The more of these things that we can throw at the political system, the better. Think of it this way—do we want a group entirely made up of lawyers to decide all of our agricultural policies? Or a bunch of people who are from rural areas making policies for big cities? Or, only older Americans without student loan debt deciding how to handle those policies? The idea is that if we have as many people as possible, from backgrounds as diverse as possible, deciding on the policies together, we will end up with the best policies that address problems more appropriately.

One might wonder how we can increase political participation in the United States. Researchers from the University of Northern Iowa, Justin Holmes and Ramona McNeal's 2018 paper for the International Journal of Public Administration in the Digital Age (Holmes and McNeal 2018) sought to find out whether modern technology can help. The advent of television may have seemed like a good thing for participation, after all, it was suddenly easier to get information to the mass public, and more information should mean higher levels of participation, right? But as Holmes and McNeal summarize, this isn't exactly what happened. In fact, the rise of television was terrible for political participation and after the 1950s we saw massive drop-offs. Some studies concluded that the form of the information was bad for participation as it trivialized major issues into little sound bites. Others, namely Robert Putnam in his seminal work Bowling Alone, find that the decline in political participation during the TV era is because people started staying home to watch it instead of going out and engaging in social and political activities.

Does this mean that the internet would work the same way? Or can we look to it as a tool to potentially motivate more Americans to participate politically? Well, as Holmes and McNeal write, the evidence is mixed. Early studies found that the internet could be useful in increasing participation by providing unlimited information at any time with just a few button clicks. Considering that a lack of knowledge about the issues and candidates is one of the reasons people don't participate, it makes sense that providing this easy access would be useful, no? Plus, much of the internet is interactive, giving people more opportunity to connect with others who have similar interests and issues. And of course, this includes giving political campaigns the opportunity to connect with voters. The problem though, is that sure, we have pretty much instant access to information about government and politics, but we also have instant access to basically everything else in the world. Could I have spent my time this morning sipping coffee and reading about the developments in Iran? Sure. But did I spend my morning sipping coffee and seeing if my taste in breakfast food predicts my Harry Potter house?[2] Yes.

Many of the studies summarized by Holmes and McNeal agree that the internet seems to reinforce dispositions that the user already has. For example, an earlier study by Holmes found that when available information increases, people who are interested in politics and in learning things use it but people who aren't interested avoid it altogether. In order to test this further, Holmes and McNeal use survey data to test the following hypotheses: 1) those who engage with politics on social media will be more likely to engage in various forms of political participation that those who do not, and 2) individuals who are predisposed to political participation will be more likely to participate if they are social media users.

The findings of this study are sort of all over the place, but interesting nonetheless. The researchers find that social media use makes it more likely that the user will go to a meeting or wear a political button, but none of the other forms of engagement. The results for the test of the second hypothesis are more expected but still relatively weak. Holmes and McNeal found that people who have high levels of political interest vote at even higher rates if they are social media users. Overall, the findings suggest that it is true that the internet, and specifically social media, increase the "you-ness" of who you already are. You love politics? Engaging on social media may make you turn out to vote. No interest at all in politics? Cool, there are plenty of baby Yoda memes out there for you to look at instead.

One phenomenon that Holmes and McNeal didn't consider is what is known as "slacktivism." Many websites and social media platforms give users the ability to feel like they are participating through mechanisms that are not the traditional outlets. "Liking", "sharing", "tweeting", joining online communities, signing online petitions, putting topical filters over a profile picture ... these are all ways that users can be made to feel like they are making a difference. And no doubt, awareness of issues and signaling support can be useful when it comes to affecting change, however critics wonder if slacktivism might serve to lessen political participation out in the real world. If a person "likes" a cause and signs a change.org petition, are they less likely to contact their member of congress? If you can subtweet the President directly, are you less likely to vote?

The internet is a behemoth of a thing and the way we use it continues to evolve over time. Can it be used to increase political participation at this point in time? Maybe a little, and maybe mostly in groups of people who are already interested in politics. But will this be the same in five years? In ten years? Probably not.

Discussion Questions

1. Why do you think young people are less likely to vote than their older peers?
2. Why should we even care about increasing participation?
3. Do you feel like your peers use the internet to gain information about current events and candidates running for election? Is this something we should try to encourage?
4. How do you feel about the idea of "slacktivism"? Is this something you witness in your life?

Key Concepts

- Political Participation
- Representative democracy

- Disenfranchisement
- Social media
- Slacktivism

For More Information:

https://www.washingtonpost.com/news/monkey-cage/wp/2014/03/12/does-slacktivism-work/?utm_term=.036bf7f55fd9

https://www.theatlantic.com/politics/archive/2018/11/youth-turnout-midterm-2018/575092/

https://www.pewresearch.org/global/2018/10/17/international-political-engagement/

Notes

1 The Hawthorne effect is when subjects of a study alter their behavior because they are aware they are being studied. This term comes from a set of experiments performed at the Hawthorne Works factory outside Chicago where they were looking at whether things like changes in the lighting would increase worker productivity. Instead, the researchers found that the workers got more productive due to the fact that they were being observed.
2 French toast and Slytherin. Accurate.

Works Cited

Department of Homeland Security. (2016, July 12). *Written testimony of NPPD for a House Homeland Security Subcommittee on Cybersecurity, Infrastructure Protection, and Security Technologies hearing titled "Value of DHS' Vulnerability Assessments in Protecting our Nation's Critical Infrastructure"*. https://www.dhs.gov/news/2016/07/12/written-testimony-nppd-house-homeland-security-subcommittee-cybersecurity

Gerber, A. S., Green, D. P., & Larimer, C. W. (2008). Social Pressure and Voter Turnout: Evidence from a Large-Scale Field Experiment. *American Political Science Review, 102*(1), 33–48. https://doi.org/10.1017/s000305540808009x

Good, C. (2018). *5 states will vote without paper ballots; experts want that to change.* ABC News. https://abcnews.go.com/Politics/states-vote-paper-ballots-experts-change/story?id=57835958

Schwartz, J. (2018, November). *The Vulnerabilities of Our Voting Machines.* Scientific American. https://www.scientificamerican.com/article/the-vulnerabilities-of-our-voting-machines/

Hegel, G., In Wood, A.W. and Nisbet, H.B. (1991). *Elements of the philosophy of right.* Cambridge University Press.

Holmes, J. W., & McNeal, R. S. (2018). Social Media Use and Political Mobilization. *International Journal of Public Administration in the Digital Age, 5*(4), 50–60. https://doi.org/10.4018/ijpada.2018100104

6

POLITICAL PARTIES
AND INTEREST GROUPS

In his 1991 book, "A Parliament of Whores: A Lone Humorist Attempts to Explain the Entire U.S. Government," author P.J. O'Rourke said, "The Democrats are the party that says government will make you smarter, taller, richer, and remove the crabgrass on your lawn. The Republicans are the party that says government doesn't work and then they get elected and prove it" (O'Rourke 2003, p. 156). This kind of cynicism abounds in discussions of political parties. And if you think Americans are cynical about political parties, they are wildly so when it comes to interest groups. Of course, a healthy level of skepticism is appropriate when it comes to the power dynamics of those running our governments and controlling our resources, however a full understanding of what these groups actually are and what power they actually wield is extremely important. This is especially true in that a belief that there are no differences between the major parties and that interest groups matter more than individual citizens contributes significantly to the decision made by more than half of Americans to not vote.

Political parties recruit candidates for offices and provide them with support for their campaigns. They give candidates money or help them to raise it and offer logistical and strategic assistance. Just as important, they help coordinate a candidate's message with those of other candidates running for other offices under the party's banner. Since the 1850s, the majority of candidates have run as members of either the Democratic or the Republican Party. Those parties as we know them now have developed and changed over time. The first part of this chapter addresses one of those big changes— how the Southern U.S. used to be solidly Democratic, but has been comfortably Republican for many years now. We will look at factors that caused the flip and some analysis of whether we ever will see it turn back the other direction.

Raising money for candidates is a huge part of the campaign and election process in the United States. Even before the Citizens United decision by the United States Supreme Court, we were seeing record amounts being raised by candidates for office, and since that ruling, well, the amount of money involved in running a national-level campaign is unfathomable to most of us. For instance, when Barack Obama ran against Mitt Romney, each of them raised over a billion dollars. That's billion with a b. And in recent years, we have seen more money that ever flowing into state and local elections as well. The second section of this chapter looks at this phenomenon, examining the reasons for the increase and discussing some of the implications.

The final section of this chapter is on interest groups, and one big one in particular: the American Legislative Exchange Council, or ALEC. Interest groups are either a necessary or a detrimental part of our policymaking process here in the United States depending on who you talk to. ALEC presents a particularly interesting case as it is extremely powerful and uses a different tactic than most other groups. Read on to consider how model bills are being used to spread corporate interests across the states.

A Two-Party System Requires Two Parties: Democrats in the South

According to legend, on July 2, 1964, after he signed the Civil Rights Act, President Lyndon B. Johnson lamented, "I think we just delivered the South to the Republican Party for a long time to come" (Oreskes 1989). Even if the direct quote has been found likely to be myth, the sentiment isn't wrong.

The Civil Rights Act put an end to legal segregation based on race, religion, or national origin in public places. This included both public areas like parks, courthouses government buildings and places that accommodate the public such as movie theaters, restaurants, and hotels. The act also banned discrimination on these factors by employers and created the Equal Employment Opportunity Commission to enforce these rules. And to go even further, the act ensured that federal funding would be withheld from any institution or program that continued to discriminate, giving the Commission on Civil Rights increased power to guarantee compliance. While civil rights legislation had been passed previously, none had been as far-reaching and comprehensive as the 1964 act. Martin Luther King Jr. reportedly even went so far as to call it a "second emancipation" (Library of Congress 2010).

So, how did this one act of law put the nail in the coffin of the Democratic Party in the South? Just follow the history of parties and racial politics in the United States.

We have not always had parties in the U.S. called the Democratic Party and the Republican Party. In fact, the Republican Party wasn't founded until 1854, a good 65 years after the Constitution was signed and the United States as we know it was made official. The Democratic Party had become the party defending the right of the southern states to maintain slavery and the Republican Party emerged as a northern party focused on anti-slavery principles.

The fight over the right to own slaves was so vicious and so all-encompassing that not only did it cause the southern states to try to leave the United States and cause a Civil War, but it also caused a political divide that lasted almost a century. Until the late 1940s or so, the Democratic hold on the South was so complete that it was basically impossible to be elected in a Southern state without that "D" behind your name. And all this time this hold was still the effect of the Civil War and the grudge the southern states had against Lincoln and the Republican Party for ending slavery.

By the Roosevelt Administration, we had started to see some movement though. FDR signed a nondiscrimination order for the national defense industry, which had never been done before. His wife even famously quit the Daughters of the American Revolution for banning black singer Marian Anderson from performing at Constitution Hall. Some of the New Deal programs really benefitted the black community, which was suffering badly during this time. These moves started to bring black Americans into the New Deal Coalition and increased their presence in the Democratic Party.

The big moment, however, came a few years later when Southern Democrat President Harry Truman introduced a civil rights platform at the 1948 Democratic convention, and a considerable faction of delegates got up and walked right out. These defectors, who called themselves "Dixiecrats" decided to take their dissatisfaction one step further, planning and holding their own, separate convention in Alabama where they nominated well-known civil rights opponent Strom Thurmond (yes, THAT Strom Thurmond. He lived for a really long time) for President. Running on a "states' rights" platform that served as an extremely thin veil for simple racism, Thurmond lost the election to Truman. He did manage, however, to win more than a million votes. This rift, over civil rights, marked the first time since 1860 that the South was not distinctly and uniformly Democratic. The beginning of the end for Southern Democrats.

And it really was only the beginning. For a while yet, most Southerners continued to vote for Democratic candidates. After all, the Republican Party was the party of Lincoln, and no one south of the Mason-Dixon Line was quite ready to forget how much they disliked Lincoln and what they felt he had done to their world. Thus, the South remained at least nominally Democratic (though increasingly supportive of conservative policies that we now think of as Republican) until 1964, and even that wasn't some sort of immediate and total change. Some Southern Democrats had already been slowly trickling over to the GOP and even through the 1960s and early 1970s, there were still white Southerners who held out as members of the Democratic Party. Heck, George Wallace, the Alabama Governor who had run for President in 1972 on a "Segregation now, segregation tomorrow, and segregation forever" (Wallace 1963) platform was running as a Democrat. For many of you reading this, 1972 probably sounds like a really long time ago, but keep this in mind: people who turned eighteen in 1972 are just now reaching retirement age.

By 1980, the country had elected Ronald Reagan as president and the Republican Party's control of the South had been solidified. It is pretty ironic considering how anti-Republican the region had been when the party started. All of those statues of Confederate war "heroes"? Largely Democrats, who would be shocked at what each of the parties looks like today.

There remain areas across the South that elect Democrats to state legislatures and occasionally to the House of Representatives. As of this writing, however, if we look at the eleven states that were part of the Confederacy plus Kentucky and Oklahoma (states considered part of the South), Republicans control ten gubernatorial offices, every state legislative chamber, and 23 of the 26 U.S. Senate seats.

So, does this mean that there is no hope for the Democratic Party to regain a foothold in the South? If history has taught us anything, it should be that we shouldn't rule anything out. And to be sure, the demographics of much of the south are changing. For example, in 2000, white voters made up more than 75% of the turnout in the Georgia election, but in 2012, that number had decreased to 61% (Georgia Secretary of State n.d.). Two different things are happening— first, many black Americans whose families had moved north during previous decades have been moving back south in higher numbers than ever. And second, Latino and Asian Americans have been moving into southern states at far higher rates than in the past. These demographic trends favor Democratic political candidates.

Areas with a relatively large minority vote that also have areas that are more suburban with higher numbers of college-educated voters are being targeted by groups like the DCCC. You see this combination in areas of Georgia, North Carolina, Florida, and Virginia, for example. That isn't to say that all highly educated, suburban, or minority voters are the same, but there are trends that would indicate that Democrats may become more competitive in these areas soon. And in Texas, where 45% of voters are non-white (Texas Politics Project n.d.) and where there are already Democratic strongholds in a couple of the urban areas (Houston and Austin, namely), many strategists see a sleeping giant.

All of this discussion of racial politics does not mean that other discussions of Southern culture are inappropriate or necessarily incorrect. Southern culture is meaningful and it is BIG. To many people who live in the South, being Southern is extremely important. And this often includes people who move to Southern states. From the food on the table, to the truck in the driveway, to the music on the radio, culture is perhaps more of an entity in the American South than in any other part of the country. And you can see this if you watch candidates run for office in these states. G's are dropped in speeches so that accents seem thicker. Guns and trucks appear in campaign ads. The God of the Christian Bible gets a copious number of shout outs. Any move toward changing the political culture, even if that change is simply nominal, won't be easily won. And considering Republicans control all of the state legislatures in the South and have been the ones drawing the district maps and controlling election rules, it is safe to say that any changes that we may see will likely be slow and sporadic.

Discussion Questions

1. Would a demographic change be the only way for Southern states to swing back toward the Democratic Party? Why or why not?
2. Do you think that most people understand that the political parties today are not the same as they were in the 1950s? Or the 1860s? Why is this?
3. Do other U.S. regions have as strong a cultural identity as southerners? Why or why not?

Key Concepts

- Republican Party
- Democratic Party
- Civil Rights Act of 1964

For More Information:

www.vox.com/policy-and-politics/2019/10/9/20900662/texas-democrats-swing-state-blue-2020

http://nymag.com/intelligencer/2018/11/changing-southern-democratic-party.html

www.nber.org/papers/w21703.pdf

(Maybe Don't) Show Me the Money: Big Money's Influence in State and Local Elections

In the current contentious U.S. political climate, concern about the influence of wealthy campaign donors on elections is growing. According to a 2016 poll, Americans believe reducing the influence of money in politics (Hensel 2016) is one of the most important issues facing the country. Despite the vitriolic rhetoric and doomsday-predicting headlines about our division as a nation, a majority of the country is largely in agreement on this topic. Over 80% of respondents agree that the influence of money in politics is worse now than at any other time in their lives. 72% back bipartisan efforts to address money in politics, and 78% favor large-scale reform that reduces the influence of money in politics (Hensel 2016).

This problem doesn't only exist at the federal level; it is also very much an issue in state and local elections. According to legend, when George Washington ran for the Virginia House of Burgesses in 1757, he spent about $200 (McCue 2019). Any more, running for state or local office is likely going to cost you quite a bit more than the price of a really good dinner party (which is what Georgie Boy spent that $200 on, though bribing voters with delicious food is no longer legal in Virginia). The amount of money raised and spent by candidates for state and local office varies widely. Many local elections really don't have any campaign spending at all, while some look more like statewide or even congressional elections. Statewide offices can vary dramatically as well, depending on the state, the level of competition, and the perception of that position's importance in the grander political scheme. There has been a trend toward those overall numbers increasing pretty dramatically, though. Some of these races make the headlines—the Los Angeles Mayoral race cost $33 million in 2013 (Moore 2013). In New York City, Michael Bloomberg spent $109 million to get reelected as mayor (Frazier 2010). And this isn't limited to the big cities either. In 2017, candidates for city council in Waterloo, Iowa raised almost $48,000 for the 2017 election, which is almost seven times what was raised during the equivalent period during the 2013 election and almost three times the previous record for amount raised (Jamison 2017).

In 2010, the U.S. Supreme Court passed Citizens United v. Federal Election Commission and its sister case, SpeechNOW v. Federal Election Commission. These cases held that the Constitution's First Amendment right to free speech means that the government cannot limit the political spending of either corporations or individuals. As a result, "Corporations, labor organizations, and political committees may make unlimited independent expenditures from their own funds, and individuals may pool unlimited funds in an independent expenditure-only political committee. It necessarily follows that corporations, labor organizations, and political committees also may make unlimited contributions to organizations such as the Committee that makes only independent expenditures" (Federal Elections Commissions n.d.-a). This ruling brought forth an outpouring of political spending, at the federal level certainly, but also at the state and local levels as some of those places adjusted their own laws to fall in line with the federal regulations.

This isn't to say that there are no restrictions at all on campaign donations at the federal level or in the states that followed suit. The Federal Election Campaign Act of 1971 (Federal Elections Commission n.d.-b) limited political contributions to candidates for federal elective office to $1,000 and by a political committee to $5,000 to any single candidate per election (the limit has been raised over time). This act was challenged in court, rising up to the U.S. Supreme Court in the case, Buckley v. Valeo (1976). The court found that even though donations were a form of free speech/expression, restrictions on large campaign contributions are justified by the state's interest in "the prevention of corruption and the appearance of corruption spawned by the real or imagined coercive influence of large financial contributions on candidates' positions and on their actions if election to office." The Court further defined "corruption" to mean "large contributions ... given to secure a political quid pro quo from current and potential office holders" (Buckley v. Valeo 1976).

Federal laws deal with the use of money in federal elections, however the states themselves create and enforce campaign finance laws for state- and local-level elections. This leads to quite a bit of variation in campaign finance laws from state-to-state. Some states, like Iowa, Nebraska, Alabama, and Utah do not have any campaign contribution limits. Donate all the money you want to whomever you choose. However, if you live in Alaska, you can only donate up to $500 per candidate per year (National Conference of State Legislators 2019).

One of the reasons that we are seeing such a spike in spending on state and local elections is the growing realization among political operatives that donating to candidates at this level has an outsized impact on policy. As much as political candidates tout the impact of small donations on their campaigns, it is often the big donors that count the most. Spending large sums on local elections is not only a way of sidestepping gridlock at the federal level, it is a more cost-effective approach to gaining political influence. A donation of $100,000 or even a million dollars is a drop in the bucket for a presidential candidate or even for most candidates for Congress, however a mayoral candidate or a candidate for a state legislator would be able to considerably increase his or her reach with a sum of this size. As Robert Lenhard, former chairman of the Federal Elections Commission said to the Wall Street Journal, "The ability to step in with a six- or seven-figure ad buy is going to be disproportionately effective on a local race" (Haddon 2015).

Power and control at the state and local levels also carry weight that often trickles upward. Consider things like districting after each Census. The state legislatures handle this. Thus, whichever party is in power after the decentennial person-count has the power and responsibility of redrawing the district lines. As we have seen in the past, this can have a tremendous impact on Congressional races. Further, many local elected officials run for higher office later. A huge chunk of the current Congress consists of people who served on their state legislatures, and many of them served locally prior to that. It makes sense, right? Many people who have the heart and guts for public service would also have the ambition to serve at higher levels. Plus, they get an automatic advantage when it comes to running in those races—many voters will already recognize their names. As a big-money donor, it makes sense to find an ambitious candidate early in their political career and follow them right up the line to higher office.

In 2017, 23 states made changes to their campaign finance laws. Additionally, several cities have made moves recently to change their own campaign finance systems. For example, Denver, Colorado is looking at placing new caps on contributions and creating a matching fund to help boost the power of smaller donors. Baltimore, Maryland is looking at a similar matching funds program, as is Portland, Oregon (National Conference of State Legislators 2018).

In contrast to most of the other states, Oregon doesn't have any campaign contribution limits either on individuals or corporations. Some people have taken advantage of this in order to use money to position themselves or their candidates for office. An example of this was seen during the 2012 mayoral race in Portland where each of the three leading candidates raised close to $1 million each—more than $2.5 million total—during the primary. Portland's mayor, Ted Wheeler, received over a million dollars himself in 2015-2016. And, of course, these numbers aren't even counting money spent on these candidates' behalf by political action committees.

Voters in Oregon did come close to employing campaign finance limits during their 1994 election. More than 70% of voters supported the measure; however, in 1997, the Oregon Supreme Court struck down the limits, ruling that the measure violated the free speech rights guaranteed by Oregon's constitution (Templeton 2018).

In 2016, a non-profit called Honest Elections took up the local campaign finance reform mantle, this time trying for a county-wide cap in Multnomah County (the county in which Portland is located). Again, the measure passed, this time with almost 90% of the vote. This was a huge success electorally. Heck, when can we ever get 90% of people to agree on anything? Unfortunately for these voters, the Portland Realtor's Association led a group of local businesses to challenge the measure and it was once again struck down, this time by a County Circuit Court Judge.

Honest Elections then appealed the Circuit Court decision to the Oregon Supreme Court using the same argument that was used at the federal level—while capping campaign contributions might limit free speech to some extent, the risk of corruption posed by NOT limiting campaign contributions is worse. Further, they hoped a local measure in Portland might present a temporary fix. They proposed an amendment to the city's charter that placed limits on the amount of funding a candidate can receive from individuals and PACs, as well as banning corporate donations. In yet another twist, Honest Elections was successful, as the Oregon Supreme Court overturned the lower court's ruling and ruled in April of 2020 that campaign contribution limits are legal in Oregon. A long and winding road indeed.

This move was not unique. In fact, state-level caps exist in 39 states, and many local governments have their own, more restrictive spending rules. This is ok at the state and local level as long as there are no state constitutional provisions that prohibit it. The federal statutes, while useful for purposes like Honest Elections' are really directed at federal elections.

And it is pretty clear what happens when you look at the effects of these laws. Only 3% of Americans are worth more than a million dollars. Of the largest political donors though, over 45% are millionaires. This "donor class" is also older, more male, and whiter than the U.S. population. This imbalance highlights the potential that policy areas that don't affect the wealthy elite might not be getting the attention they merit. One might wonder how this jibes with the idea of "one person, one vote."

Discussion Questions

1. Should there be limits on campaign spending? What are the pros and cons?
2. Do you agree that campaign donations are a form of free speech? Why or why not?
3. Look back at the Buckley v. Valeo ruling. What do you think of the idea that free speech can be overwritten by the potential risks?

Key Concepts

- Campaign finance reform
- Citizens United v. Federal Election Commission
- Buckley v. Valeo
- Census

For More Information

https://ballotpedia.org/Costs_of_administering_local_elections
www.oyez.org/cases/1975/75-436
www.ncsl.org/research/elections-and-campaigns/election-costs-who-pays-and-with-which-funds.aspx

ALEC and the Use and Misuse of Model Bills

If you look closely you might notice that many of the bills proposed and passed in state legislatures across the country look similar. Sometimes more than similar—identical. This is no amazing coincidence brought about by the great minds of elected officials thinking alike. Instead, we are seeing the pervasive trend of legislators using model bills. Model bills are policy drafts, or templates, written by outside groups to be used by lawmakers around the country. One such group that has been particularly prolific in terms of writing these bills and getting them passed by state legislatures from coast to coast is the American Legislative Exchange Council.

This conservative organization generally flies under the radar of the average American, however their reach and influence are extensive. The American Legislative Exchange Council (better known as ALEC) was founded in September of 1973 by a group of state legislators including Henry Hyde, Paul Weyrich, and Lou Barnett. Weyrich in particular had been a key player in conservative politics and was also involved in the founding of the Heritage Foundation right around this same time and later went on to found other conservative think tanks like the Free Congress Foundation. ALEC's mission is to "advance limited government, free markets, and federalism at the state level through a nonpartisan public-private partnership of America's state legislators, members of the private sector and the general public" (American Legislative Exchange Council). Specifically, they work toward this mission by linking state legislators to corporations and creating templates for state legislation. They have worked with corporations such as ExxonMobil, Koch Industries, and Reynolds Tobacco among many others to achieve their goals.

ALEC has developed model legislation on a wide range of topics of interest to corporate and conservative stakeholders, and supporting lawmakers in many states have introduced and passed many of these bills. For example, one of ALEC's most well-known model bills is the "Castle Doctrine," otherwise known as the "Stand Your Ground" bill. Back in 2012, a Florida man, George Zimmerman shot and killed an unarmed teenager named Trayvon Martin who had gone out in his father's neighborhood to buy snacks at a local convenience store. In the immediate aftermath of the shooting, the police declined to arrest Zimmerman, as the reasons he gave for the shooting ostensibly fell within the bounds of the Florida version of the ALEC bill. Eventually, the national attention and outrage was enough that Zimmerman was charged with murder. At the trial, the jury was informed of the law, under which Zimmerman had no duty to retreat, and in fact was permitted to use deadly force if he felt threatened. He was acquitted. This incident and the attention it gained nationally stands out, however it is not alone. As the Center for Media and Democracy published in a report later that year, the National Rifle Association was instrumental in the drafting of the Florida Stand Your Ground law, which then was proposed as an ALEC model bill by an NRA lobbyist during a 2005 ALEC conference. ALEC adopted and distributed the bill, and at the time of Treyvon Martin's death, 23 states had adopted it as well (Reeve 2012).

Not all of ALEC's model bills are quite as flashy though. In March of 2012, the Iowa Senate passed Senate File 376, a bill significantly restricting lawsuits by people who have suffered asbestos-related injuries. The bill's introduction struck some Senators as odd, as there was no evidence that there had ever been a problem with the way these lawsuits were handled in Iowa. But there was no mystery afoot. A few years earlier, ALEC had adopted a model bill, The Asbestos Claims Transparency Act, using virtually the same language. Since then, identical (or nearly so) bills have sprung up around the country in places like Ohio, Oklahoma, Louisiana, and Texas (Petroski 2017).

There is nothing illegal or even unethical about ALEC's methods. It does bring up some serious questions though. Take the Asbestos Claims Transparency Act. Exposure to asbestos causes many health problems, the most common of which is a specific, extremely dangerous type of lung cancer called mesothelioma. Around 3,000 cases of mesothelioma are diagnosed every year. Further, it turns out that the risk involved in asbestos exposure has been known for many, many years and that there had been negligent disregard for the health and wellbeing of those who work around asbestos by many companies. So, there are lawsuits. Lots and lots of lawsuits. Brought against these companies that allowed their employees to be exposed to asbestos even while knowing that it was bad for them.

It is extremely expensive to be sued. It is even more expensive to be sued over and over again. Many of the companies involved ended up filing for bankruptcy with the caveat that they set aside trust funds to handle future asbestos claims. This is also extraordinarily pricey. It is perhaps unsurprising then that many of ALEC's corporate sponsors who have been held liable for asbestos-related injuries in the past showed support for the model legislation. And maybe even less surprising that even a cursory glance at the donor lists for the legislators who supported the bill in their own state include many of those same ALEC corporate sponsors. In the Iowa case, the Senator who introduced the bill has listed as his major campaign contributors more than one company that has been affected by asbestos lawsuits. This is not necessarily to suggest that something untoward is going on. Corporate campaign contributions are ubiquitous in the United States. However, the bill's sponsor is a member of ALEC, and ALEC's goal is to match business with legislators and create model legislation to link the two. Mission accomplished.

This is not to say that all model legislation is bad or that it is only used for shady economic benefits and corporate interests. Many organizations develop language that is based on their expertise in a certain subject so that policymakers might have an easier time writing a bill or a rule. You can do an internet search on many different policy areas and type, "model bill" after it and come up with sample legislation written by groups attempting to be helpful or hoping to influence a particular area. For instance, a search on "model student dress code policy" brings up the National Organization of Women's Oregon chapter. This group recognized that dress codes around the country have been criticized for reinforcing gender stereotypes and for not being culturally or religiously inclusive. They propose a policy that addresses these criticisms. Or search "model legislation bike lanes" and you will get a link to the League of American Bicyclists. This group, which has been around since 1880, has a legislative affairs committee that studied best practices on bike safety from around the country that has put together four different bike-related model laws for use by anyone who wants to use them. While both of these groups certainly have a perspective in mind that not everyone will necessarily agree with, it is pretty safe to say that neither is out to gain anything inappropriately through use of their model work.

This is also not to say that it is necessarily a bad thing to protect the interests of businesses. Corporations and small businesses are vital to the functioning of the United States. They provide jobs, create products, and contribute to the economy in ways that individual Americans cannot. We absolutely should be creating a business-friendly environment, and sometimes that means that we have to make trade-offs. Take the environment, for example. Regulations that help keep the air and water clean are often expensive for companies in certain industries. Further, many of these regulations and projects are expensive for governments to institute. One of ALEC's model bills, "The Environmental Priorities Act" acknowledges both the importance of environmental stewardship and the costs involved for both corporations and the government. They propose creating state-level councils containing representatives from government, the corporate world, and the environmental science world to systematically prioritize proposals regarding the environment. Involving business interests in decisions about environmental policy is not everyone's cup of tea, and that is ok. You might not like dress codes or bike lanes either. And not even all of ALEC's model bills are for the interests of corporations (though remember, that IS their mission as an organization). One of their model bills, The Civic Literacy Act (American Legislative Exchange Council n.d.), would require teaching the Constitution, Declaration of Independence, and Federalist Papers in High School. This isn't exactly controversial or politically divisive for most Americans.

Whether you agree with the content of model bills put out by organizations like ALEC though is a little beside the point. One of the benefits of a federal system of government such as the one we have in the United States is that we elect representatives at the state and local level that are supposed to be more tuned in to the interests of the people in that area, and that those interests may be different from people who live in a different state. When a powerful interest group spends a lot of time and money pushing identical policy across many locations, a challenge for both federalism and for representative government is presented.

Discussion Questions

1. Are there other groups out there doing work similar to ALEC? Any that approach the level of influence?

2. Should model bills be illegal? Why or why not?
3. What are the risks involved in letting an outside organization write legislation?

Key Concepts

* American Legislative Exchange Council
* Model bills

For More Information

www.alec.org/
www.desmoinesregister.com/story/news/politics/2019/04/04/iowa-model-legislation-alec-alice-special-interest-groups-state-law-asbestos-campus-workers-reynolds/3346686002/
www.usatoday.com/story/news/investigations/2019/04/03/alec-american-legislative-exchange-council-model-bills-republican-conservative-devos-gingrich/3162357002/

Works Cited

American Legislative Exchange Council. (n.d.). *Civic Literacy Act* - www.alec.org. Retrieved October 14, 2020, from https://www.alec.org/model-policy/the-civic-literacy-act/

American Legislative Exchange Council. (2016). *Strategic Plan.* https://www.alec.org/app/uploads/2016/06/ALEC-Strat-Plan-Final-051616.pdf

Federal Elections Commission. (n.d.-a). *Making independent expenditures.* FEC.Gov. Retrieved October 14, 2020, from https://www.fec.gov/help-candidates-and-committees/making-independent-expenditures/

Federal Elections Commission. (n.d.-b). *Appendix 4: Brief History.* Transition.Fec.Gov. Retrieved October 14, 2020, from https://transition.fec.gov/info/appfour.htm

Frazier, S. K. (2010). *Bloomberg Spent $109M To Barely Win a Third Term.* NBC New York. https://www.nbcnewyork.com/news/local/bloomberg-spent-109m-to-barely-win-a-third-term/1915254/

Georgia Secretary of State. (n.d.). *Voter Turn Out By Demographics | Elections.* Sos.Ga.Gov. Retrieved October 14, 2020, from https://sos.ga.gov/index.php/Elections/voter_turn_out_by_demographics

Haddon, H. (2015, October 19). Super PACs Target Local Races. *Wall Street Journal.* https://www.wsj.com/articles/super-pacs-target-local-races-1445216030

Hensel, D. (2016). *Issue One – New Poll Shows Money in Politics Is A Top Voting Concern.* Issue One. https://www.issueone.org/new-poll-shows-money-in-politics-is-a-top-voting-concern/

Jamison, T. (2017). *Waterloo council races see big money raised and spent.* Waterloo Cedar Falls Courier. https://wcfcourier.com/news/local/govt-and-politics/waterloo-council-races-see-big-money-raised-and-spent/article_2007ee52-359b-5ce8-97f4-6b373e92ad1b.html

Library of Congress. (2010). *Civil Rights Era (1950–1963) - The Civil Rights Act of 1964: A Long Struggle for Freedom | Exhibitions - Library of Congress*. Loc.Gov. https://www.loc.gov/exhibits/civil-rights-act/civil-rights-era.html

McCue, D. (2019). *George Washington to Citizens United: A History of Campaign Finance Reform*. Commoncause.Org. https://www.commoncause.org/democracy-wire/george-washington-to-citizens-united-a-history-of-campaign-finance-reform/

Moore, M. (2013, May 19). *Campaign spending sets record*. Los Angeles Times. https://www.latimes.com/archives/la-xpm-2013-may-18-la-me-mayor-money-20130519-story.html

National Conference of State Legislators. (2018). *2017 Campaign Finance Enactments*. NCSL. https://www.ncsl.org/research/elections-and-campaigns/2017-campaign-finance-enactments.aspx

National Conference of State Legislators. (2019). *State Limits on Contributions to Candidates*. NCSL. https://www.ncsl.org/research/elections-and-campaigns/state-limits-on-contributions-to-candidates.aspx

Oreskes, M. (1989, July 2). Civil Rights Act Leaves Deep Mark On the American Political Landscape. *The New York Times*. https://www.nytimes.com/1989/07/02/us/civil-rights-act-leaves-deep-mark-on-the-american-political-landscape.html

O'Rourke, P. J. (2003). *Parliament of Whores: a lone humorist attempts to explain the entire U.S. government*. Grove Pr., Cop.

Petroski, W. (2017). *Bill restricting asbestos victims' claims gets Iowa Senate OK after heated debate*. Des Moines Register. https://www.desmoinesregister.com/story/news/politics/2017/03/08/bill-restricting-asbestos-victims-claims-gets-iowa-senate-ok-after-heated-debate/98899762/

Reeve, E. (2012, April 17). *ALEC, Group That Pushed Stand Your Ground, Quits the Culture Wars*. The Atlantic. https://www.theatlantic.com/politics/archive/2012/04/alec-group-pushed-stand-your-ground-quits-culture-wars/329233/

Templeton, A. (2018). *Portland voters Pass campaign finance limits*. OPB. https://www.opb.org/news/article/portland-oregon-election-campaign-finance-result/

Texas Politics Project. (n.d.). *Texas Politics - The Demographics of Voting*. https://texaspolitics.utexas.edu/archive/html/vce/features/0302_02/demographics.html

Wallace, G. (1963). *Inaugural Address*. https://digital.archives.alabama.gov/digital/collection/voices/id/2952

7

STATE LEGISLATURES

Legislatures have one of the toughest jobs in the political system. It is difficult to get my family to agree on where we should have dinner, much less get dozens, or even hundreds, to agree on something controversial like abortion or welfare. And they do this over and over during their sessions. And ultimately there will always be people who are unhappy with the choices that you made.

Historically, state legislatures, like the U.S. Congress, have been largely made up of white men. This has started to change. The number of women, for instance, has increased pretty steadily over the past few decades, which may lead you to wonder if it matters. Does it make a difference, policy wise, when there are more women making laws? Well, that's a question we tackle in the first section. Then we move to the ins and outs of professional, full-time state legislatures versus those that meet more sporadically. Finally, we leap to a topic that is more … ripped from the headlines, if you will: Jeffrey Epstein. Specifically, we take a look at how variation in state laws may have amplified his ability to get away with crimes.

Descriptive Representation and Policy Outcomes: Do Female Legislators Matter?

In December 2018, the Clark County Board of County Commissioners in Nevada appointed Beatrice Duran and Rochelle Thuy Nguyen to the two vacant Las Vegas-area seats in the State Assembly. This is routine. Sometimes people decide to leave office before election time, sometimes elected officials pass away. But this time, in Nevada, the appointment of these two women made history. Nevada became the first state to have a majority female legislature.

Before these appointments, the Nevada assembly was already doing pretty well in terms of gender parity, with women comprising a full 50% of its membership. Nationwide, the share of women legislators is just over 28%, itself a major improvement from before the 2018 elections when women only made up 25% of the state legislators (which is still pretty good compared to the 4% of seats women held in 1971). In individual states, few approach parity. Colorado's House of Representatives is 50% female. Back in the 2009-2010 session, the New Hampshire Senate had a female majority too.

You may be reading this thinking, cool, but it doesn't matter. Men and women should be able to govern equally well so gender doesn't matter. But maybe it does. Descriptive representation is the notion that elected representatives should represent their constituents on policy positions but also on things like gender, ethnicity, religion, or other descriptive characteristics that might have political implications. This is based on the assumption that individuals who share descriptive characteristics also share common interests and that if you elect one of these individuals to office, that person will enact policies that will benefit others who share those characteristics. The idea is that there are distinct life experiences that go along with particular characteristics that make a representative more likely to view policy in a way that is in line with others who share that characteristic. For example, women may have distinct childbearing and rearing experiences that are different from their male counterparts.

There have been many studies examining whether there is a relationship between descriptive representation and policies that benefit the group with that characteristic. Do female representatives "stand for" women? The answer to this question is sort of mixed. Research has indicated that yes, women do have different policy preferences and priorities than men do (remember, we are talking on average here), but that this does not always translate to actual policy implementation. It turns out that it is just more complicated than simply saying that electing more women will necessarily mean that a legislative body will enact more women-friendly policies.

In 2017, researchers Marie Courtemanche and Joanne Connor Green published an article, "The Influence of Women Legislators on State Health Care Spending for the Poor" in the journal Social Sciences (Courtemanche and Green 2017). They argued that because there weren't any legislative bodies where women held majority status that their ability to truly influence policy in favor of their group interest was limited. Indeed, it is difficult to sway the agenda when your issue is only prioritized by a minority. Thus, they contend that descriptive representation would increase when the topic at hand is something that is easily framed as an important issue that would impact a lot of people.

In order to test this, Courtenmanche and Green look at welfare policies that affect children, the elderly, and the disabled. Both as individuals and as caregivers, these policies disproportionately affect women and the researchers expected that female legislators, regardless of political party, would be especially attuned to these issues and more likely to support policies that devote more resources to the related programs than their male legislative counterparts. Healthcare spending, they posit, is an issue that is pretty obviously an important issue. They note that Medicaid, which pays for the bulk of these programs, is the single largest state expenditure around the country and that it is increasing all the time. By their logic, then, an increase in the female proportion of a legislature should increase spending on healthcare for children, the elderly, and the disabled.

The researchers looked at all 50 states for the off-numbered years between 1999 and 2009 and at the variation in both their independent variable and a handful of dependent variables. Their independent variable (the one that they are hypothesizing is driving the change in the other variables), is women's descriptive representation—what percentage of the state's legislature is made up of women. Then they look at how that variable is related to spending on children's healthcare programs, spending on home healthcare for the elderly and disabled, and Medicaid spending per enrollee. Remember from Chapter 1, it is the variation in these numbers that allows us to compare and contrast how things are working.

The study finds that merely increasing the percentage of women in a state's legislature does not increase spending on these welfare programs. This was not exactly surprising to the researchers though. Remember, in order to pass a policy, you generally need at least half, sometimes 2/3 of the body to vote for it, and women had not yet been elected to any legislature in those numbers. The researchers did find though that when a higher percentage of female legislators is found together with a state population that has an increasing need for a policy that spending on that policy did increase. In other words, as the number of poor children in a state increases, having more female legislators means you are more likely to see an increase in spending for children's healthcare. This was the same for expenditures on vulnerable adults. If you have an increasing population of elderly and disabled adults, having more female legislators leads to higher spending levels. If you flip it, and have a growing need from these groups but few women in the legislature, the research found that you would actually see a decrease in spending for that group.

One of the implications from this research is that when there is a great need for programmatic support, women in legislatures are able to convince some of their male counterparts to align with them in increasing spending. Considering there has never been a state legislature in the U.S. where women make up over half of the members, this alignment has so far been necessary. In Nevada, though the total number of women in the legislature is more than half (32 out of 63), they only hold an actual majority in the Assembly (23 of 42 members) and not in the Senate (nine of 21), so we still won't see what the policy effects would be if women held majorities in both houses. However, considering the unprecedented number of women who ran for office in the 2018 election, it is easy to imagine that this may change sooner rather than later. It will be interesting to see whether a continuing increase in women representatives will translate to further increases in spending for programs like healthcare.

Discussion Questions

1. It is surprising to you that it wasn't until 2018 that a state had a majority female legislature?
2. Are there other groups that if more represented in lawmaking bodies, would make a difference in the type of policies that are enacted?
3. Is it more important to try to vote for a diverse group of lawmakers so that everyone gets represented, or to simply look at the candidate and their policy preferences?

Key Concepts

- Descriptive representation
- Substantive representation

For More Information:

www.leg.state.nv.us/Division/Research/Publications/Bkground/BP95-01.pdf
https://journals-sagepub-com.proxy.lib.uni.edu/doi/pdf/10.1177/1065912910376388

Professional Versus Citizen Legislatures

Ben Kieckhefer is a state Senator in Nevada. He is also the director of client relations for McDonald Carano, a high-profile law firm that represents some pretty big clients. This isn't unusual. In fact, most states have "part-time" legislatures where the scope of the work expected from the members and the paychecks they receive require most members to maintain outside employment.

The concept of "citizen legislatures" is really popular around the country. The notion that lawmakers should be regular Joes with jobs and live outside the capitol building rather than being professional politicians reflects the value that many Americans place on elected officials being able to relate to the real-world concerns of their constituents. 40 states have legislatures like this, ones that are considered less than full time.

The structure of legislatures reflects how a state has historically valued different types of governance and the role that the government should play in the lives of its constituents. There are part-time bodies, ones like Nevada's, where lawmakers maintain their previous employment and connection to the communities they serve. There are hybrid legislatures where the workload is larger but most lawmakers continue to work outside of their chamber. And there are a handful of full-time legislatures where members devote the majority of their time to the business of the state.

When political scientists talk about this variation, we tend to use the term "legislative professionalism" or "legislative capacity", and the fulltime-ness of the body is just one aspect of how legislatures are categorized. You can also look at how much the members are paid, for example. There is a wide range here. Members of the California legislature make $110,459, while those in New Mexico don't receive a salary and are simply paid $161 per day that they are in session and members in New Hampshire earn just $200 for their two-year term (Ballotpedia 2020). You can also look at staffing levels. On average, full-time legislators have about nine staff members working for them, while in hybrid legislatures members have about three and in part-time bodies, each member only gets one.

This is not to say that "professionalism" or "capacity" is the same as performance. In fact, the legislature in the U.S. with the highest levels of professionalism/capacity is the U.S. Congress ... and well, in recent years, the productivity of that body has been lacking. For example, in the 113th Congress, 352 bills and resolutions were passed by both chambers (though not necessarily signed into law) (*H.J. Res. 59 (113th): Continuing Appropriations Resolution*, 2014). In that same time period, the states passed 45,564—38 states plus the Washington, D.C. passed more legislation than Congress. While this is not a perfect measure of performance by any means, it does help illustrate the point. There is more to assessing how well a legislative body performs than simply looking at its levels of professionalism/capacity.

Indeed, there are pros and cons to everything. Professionalized legislatures and their higher salaries tend to attract better qualified members and those members stick around longer, leading to more experience and the opportunity to master legislative skills. They are able to focus on their legislative activities rather than spreading their attention around, which often means increased time to develop policy and then deliberate on it. High-capacity legislatures also have more staff and resources, which allows the legislator a higher capacity for policymaking.

But of course, this version of governance costs money. Higher salaries and more staff often mean higher taxes and, in general, the states with full-time legislatures have higher effective tax rates than those with part-time ones. And in addition to being less expensive, there are other advantages to less professionalized legislative bodies. For one, legislators who aren't tied to the capitol fulltime have more time to spend in their communities. This means that the legislators may have the opportunity to get to know the people and issues better.

And while fulltime legislatures have less turnover and more experience, shaking things up can lead to new, fresh ideas. Further, this more regular changing of the guard often attracts members who have a mind toward public service rather than political power.

This brings us back to Senator Kieckhefer. State legislators have a wide berth to propose and vote on laws that affect the people and industries in their states, and this includes people and industries that the legislator may have personal involvement with. In most states, the ethics rules don't require a lawmaker to necessarily recuse themselves in these cases. In fact, two states, Oregon and Utah, even require all legislators to vote on bills, even if they do have a conflict of interest. Other states have more complicated rules. In Louisiana, a legislator can participate in legislation that benefits themselves as long as they aren't the only one benefitting, for example, while in California, a legislator only has to recuse themselves if they have more than $2,000 investment in a property or business that will benefit.

Senator Kieckhefer's law firm represents a number of big clients with a number of big interests. And in several cases, Senator Kieckhefer voted to advance measures that would benefit those clients and their interests. In the most high profile of these instances, the law firm McDonald Carano (Kieckhefer's employer, remember) was representing the Oakland Raiders in their effort to get a $750 million public financing deal to relocate to Las Vegas and build a fancy new stadium. In Nevada, the usual rule is that if a legislator has a conflict of interest, they are supposed to disclose it before voting on the measure. So, it isn't that they have to abstain, just that they have to disclose the conflict. Needless to say, Kieckhefer voted to approve the financing and the Raiders moved to Las Vegas. And this is perfectly in line with the laws of Nevada and many other states (Whyte and Foley 2017).

Some states are taking measures to cut off some of these conflicts of interest. The Alaskan Legislature, for example, recently passed House Bill 44 toughening the rules on financial conflicts, gifts from lobbyists, reimbursement for foreign travel, and campaign spending by corporations from outside the country (Brooks 2019). The legislature did this in response to a petition signed by more than 40,000 Alaska citizens to put a similar law on the ballot directly. The writing was on the wall, and judging by how popular this move was with Alaska citizens, perhaps this isn't the last move like this that we will see.

Discussion Questions

1. People who are entrenched in an industry tend to know more about that industry than outsiders, but they might also be improperly biased when it comes to policymaking. How should voters assess this tension when they go to the ballot box?

2. What are the pros and cons of having a professionalized legislature versus a citizen legislature? Which would you prefer your state to have?
3. Should there be stricter rules about when a lawmaker is required to recuse themselves from voting on topics related to their citizen job?
4. What if it isn't a job that is creating a potential conflict of interest, but an investment. Should lawmakers have to recuse themselves from votes based on investments?

Key Concepts

- Citizen legislature
- Hybrid legislature
- Professional legislature
- Legislative capacity
- Legislative professionalism
- Conflict of interest

For More Information:

https://psmag.com/news/conflicts-of-interest-in-state-legislatures
https://ncsl.typepad.com/the_thicket/2013/02/full-time-or-part-time-legislature-which-is-better.html
www.ncsl.org/Portals/1/Documents/magazine/articles/2013/SL_0113-Stats.pdf

Jeffrey Epstein and the Varying Interpretation of Federal Sex Offender Registry Laws

In 2010, Jeffrey Epstein, a high-dollar investor and financier, pleaded guilty to two felony sex offenses in Florida. The crime was having sexual relations with a 17-year-old girl (the age of consent in Florida is 18 if the partner is older than 23) and solicitation. As part of his punishment, Epstein was required to register as a sex offender. This is hardly unusual—since 1994, there has been a federal statute that makes it so that all 50 states maintain a sex offender registry and track the location of those on the list. In Epstein's case though, it is more complicated and highlights some of the problems with the current system.

The federal requirement that each state implement a sex offender registry leaves a considerable amount of discretion about what the registries look like, what the requirements are for the offender, and how they are enforced varies widely between these places. Remember back to the chapter on federalism? This type of policymaking is in line with the wave of new federalism that we saw from the early 1980s to the early 2000s. The idea was that the federal government could be helpful in certain areas but that states should shoulder the responsibility for the bulk of the specific policymaking.

In some places, registered offenders are required to check in frequently, while in others an offender simply has to verify their contact information occasionally. In many states, sex offenders must report where they are working, living, and going to school. Homeless offenders in Kansas are required to report in every three days. If a registered sex offender is moving to another state, they must notify the local police, and in Maine, for example, this must be done within 24 hours (Shim 2014).

Failure to comply with the local rules is taken very seriously in some states, including felony charges, but in some states, the regulation tends to be more lax. How long you have to register for and whether or not you can ever get off the registry (and how difficult that process is) varies widely. Some states are very strict: California, Hawaii, and South Carolina all require sex offenders to stay on the registry for the rest of their lives, regardless of what the crime was. In Missouri, on the other hand, if you were under 21 and convicted of engaging in consensual sex with someone over the age of 14, you might be able to get off the registry after only two years because of a special "Romeo and Juliet" law (Shim 2014).

Jeffrey Epstein, now deceased, owned several homes around the U.S., including ones in Florida, New York, New Mexico, and the Virgin Islands. Following his conviction in 2010, he registered as a sex offender in Florida. Shortly thereafter, he registered in New York as well. New York has a requirement that those on the registry have to check in to the local police department every 90 days. Epstein never had to do this though, as right before that first 90 days were up, he officially changed his permanent address to his residence in the Virgin Islands. While in the Virgin Islands, though he was on the sex offender registry, Epstein was able to avoid much of the routine monitoring because he owned an entire island and wouldn't allow investigators to dock there.

Epstein also maintained a 26,000 square foot house, called Zorro Ranch, outside of Santa Fe, New Mexico. In the wake of the scandal surrounding his arrest and death, it came to light that Epstein was not on the sex offender registry in New Mexico due to differences in states laws about how registries are managed and what is considered a sex crime. Though Epstein had been accused of crimes involving several underage girls, the charges that he pleaded guilty to involved only one victim—a 17-year-old. In Florida, this is a crime, however in New Mexico, the age of consent is 16 so it isn't a crime for an adult in their 50s to have sex with a 17-year-old.

States-rights advocates are adamant that the specifics about how to handle things like sex offender registries should stay out of the hands of the federal government and be left to the discretion of the states, and there are certainly benefits to this. States differ in their topography, demographics, population density, and capacity to handle things like reporting and check-ins for offenders. Letting each state design a program that works for them is responsive to those issues and tends to be popular with voters who prefer policy to stay close to home. On the other hand, though, the Epstein case illustrates one of the major drawbacks—in an age where many people are able to move around the country with relative ease, might some seize upon the variation in policy and use it to their own advantage?

Discussion Questions

1. Does this case serve as an example of why these kinds of laws should be handled at the federal level or is it just one of those unfortunately casualties of federalism?
2. Should the minimum age for consent be raised at the federal level or should these kinds of decisions be left to the states?
3. Are laws requiring registered sex offenders to check in often overly burdensome on poor people?

Key Concepts

* Federalism
* Federal Sex Offender Registry
* Compliance
* Variance

For More Information:

https://www.csom.org/pubs/twenty_strategies.pdf
https://www.nytimes.com/2019/07/11/us/jeffrey-epstein-house-new-mexico.html
https://slate.com/news-and-politics/2014/08/sex-offender-registry-laws-have-our-policies-gone-too-far.html

Works Cited

Ballotpedia. (2020). *Comparison of state legislative salaries.* https://ballotpedia.org/Comparison_of_state_legislative_salaries#:~:text=In%20California%2C%20legislators%20are%20paid

Brooks, J. (2019, April 9). *Alaska House agrees with Senate on rolling back Legislative ethics law.* Anchorage Daily News. https://www.adn.com/politics/alaska-legislature/2019/04/09/alaska-house-agrees-with-senate-on-rolling-back-legislative-ethics-law/

Courtemanche, M., & Green, J. (2017). The Influence of Women Legislators on State Health Care Spending for the Poor. *Social Sciences, 6*(2), 40. https://www.mdpi.com/2076-0760/6/2/40

H.J.Res. 59 (113th): Continuing Appropriations Resolution, (2014) (testimony of Harold Rogers). Retrieved from https://www.congress.gov/congressional-report/113th-congress/house-report/306/1.

Shim, J. (2014, August 13). *These States Stick People With a Lifetime of Restrictions for Decades-Old, Nonviolent Sex Offenses*. Slate Magazine; Slate. https://slate.com/news-and-politics/2014/08/sex-offender-registry-laws-by-state-mapped.html

Whyte, L. E., & Foley, R. (2017). *State lawmakers blur line between public, personal interests*. Reno Gazette Journal. https://www.rgj.com/story/news/politics/2017/12/06/state-lawmakers-blur-line-between-public-personal-interests/926914001/

8

STATE EXECUTIVE LEADERSHIP

Governors are the prime political actors in virtually every state. Some are notably more successful than others, but all are seen as leaders. In most states, the governor sets the agenda, largely determining which policy issues will be pursued and how the state budget will look. They are unique among state-level politicians in terms of the media attention they can attract. This helps them promote their causes, but they must rely on other institutional players if they are going to accomplish more than making speeches.

Historically, governors held little real power and were basically just figureheads. Over time, they were given more formal control over the machinery of government, while at the same time the federal government shifted more power back to the states. They have longer terms than they used to (NH and VT still have two-year terms but everyone else gets a four-year term at this point).

Governors are expected to be the leaders for their states, but sometimes it doesn't work out like that. This chapter begins with the worst-case scenarios—impeachment. Impeachment is the political and administrative punishment that governors risk, but there are also benefits that come with the governor's office. One benefit is the incumbency advantage, meaning that once you have the job you are more likely to be elected to the job again. We look at why that is and whether it has changed over time.

For the last section, we look at state executive leadership in terms of how sometimes one particular governor will try to make great big strides forward, even if the national leadership isn't on board. We focus here on California and Jerry Brown's attempts to manage environmental policy and how the federal government under President Trump is working to roll all of it back.

When It All Goes Wrong: The Impeachments of Governor Robert Bently and Eric Greitens

Impeachment. A word that signals the worst possible outcome for an elected official. But it is also a complicated political process that is often misunderstood by the public.

An impeachment is the process by which an elected official is tried by other elected officials for the purpose of removing them from office. What, specifically, someone can be impeached for varies a bit depending on the laws governing the body, but generally there are provisions for impeaching an officer for incompetence or for malfeasance. The definition of those terms often falls to the body in charge of the trial—for instance, what are the "high crimes and misdemeanors" for which a President can be impeached? The Constitution doesn't say, and thus it is up to Congress to decide what they feel is an impeachable offense. This is one of the major ways in which impeachment is a political tool rather than simply an administrative or judicial one.

This holds true in the states as well. In all of the states in the U.S., save for Oregon, a governor can be impeached by the state legislature. In most states, the process is quite a bit like that used for impeachments of presidents at the federal level. If the lower chamber of the state legislature votes to impeach, then the upper chamber votes on whether or not to convict the governor, removing them from office. There are a few exceptions. In Alaska, it is the upper chamber that votes to impeach the governor while the lower chamber votes on whether or not to convict and remove. In California, the whole process is handled by the state Senate, which votes both to impeach and to convict. In Oklahoma, an impeached governor is tried before both chambers of the state Legislature in a joint session. In Nebraska, after the unicameral votes in favor of impeachment, the governor is tried by the Nebraska Supreme Court. Finally, and most unusually, in Missouri impeachments are tried by a panel seven specially-selected judges (Ballotpedia n.d.).

In the history of the United States, there are only sixteen cases of a vote being carried out to impeach a governor. Of those, nine led to the impeached governor's removal from office. The National Conference of State Legislatures suggests two potential reasons why gubernatorial impeachments are relatively uncommon; the perception that impeachment is a drastic measure and the likelihood of officers resigning before they can be impeached (National Conference of State Legislators n.d.).

Considering how rare all of this is, it is noteworthy that since 2017, two different governors have resigned in the face of impeachment trials.

In April 2017, Alabama Governor Robert Bentley resigned from office as part of a plea agreement on two misdemeanor charges: failing to file a major contribution report and knowingly converting campaign contributions to personal use. But this was only part of the story, which began (at least publicly), when First Lady Dianne Bentley abruptly filed for divorce from the Governor in late August 2015 (Blinder 2017).

Within days of the announcement by Dianne Bentley, Representative Allen Farley filed paperwork with the state Attorney General's office requesting an investigation into whether state funds were inappropriately used by the Governor. No investigation was done at this time; however, the next six months were full of salacious rumors flying around. Accusations that the Governor had been conducting an affair with an employee and using state funds to cover it up began to bubble up and by the end of March, Governor Bentley was forced to hold a press conference at which he denied carrying on a physical relationship with the employee or using any state funds inappropriately.

The press conference might have been more effective had recordings of sexual conversations with the employee not leaked on the same day. At this point, the State Auditor got involved and filed a report with the State Ethics Commission requesting an investigation into the alleged misuse of state funds, to which the Commission agreed this time. On March 30, 2016, State Representative Ed Henry announced that he would introduce articles of impeachment against Bentley, who held another press conference saying that he hadn't done anything wrong and did not intend to resign.

At this point, the State Ethics Commission is doing their investigation and the articles of impeachment have been filed. These are two separate things, conducted by two different branches of government, and come November, a third entity got involved. Attorney General Luther Strange sent a letter to members of the House Judiciary Committee to inform them of "related work" being performed by the attorney general's office and at Strange's request, the committee suspended its impeachment investigation. Three months later, Governor Bentley appointed Attorney General Strange to the U.S. Senate to replace Jeff Sessions who had become the U.S. Attorney General.

On April 6th, 2017, the State Ethics Commission released a finding of probable cause that Bentley had violated the state's ethics and campaign finance laws, and four days later, new impeachment proceedings against Bentley began. That very afternoon, April 10, 2017, Bentley was booked in the Montgomery County Jail on two misdemeanor charges of campaign finance violations.

You might wonder why having an affair is such a big deal and why it has anything to do with campaign finance. Well, having an affair is not, on its face, illegal. What Governor Bentley did wrong in a legal sense, was pay for things to facilitate the affair with money that was not his to spend in that way. He purchased cell phones and gave his mistress rides on official state planes and helicopters. He also took her along on a trip to a conference in Las Vegas. There are very strict rules on how state money and how campaign money can be spent. Suffice it to say, Celine Dion concerts are not on this list.

Impeachment is an administrative and political punishment. Charges brought by the Attorney General's office as a result of an ethics investigation can have criminal or civil implications. In this case, Bentley pleaded guilty to the criminal charges and avoided impeachment by resigning from office.

Meanwhile in Missouri …

In 2015, a seemingly perfect candidate declared himself in the running to be the next Governor of Missouri. Eric Greitens was a local boy made good with a full-ride to Duke, a major in ethics, a Rhodes Scholarship, bronze star and purple heart honors during his time as a Navy SEAL, a prestigious fellowship at the White House, a non-profit to help veterans … he seemed poised to rise rapidly through the political quagmire. He had, in fact, reserved ericgreitensforpresident.com way back in 2009, way before he had ever even run for office of any kind (Cooperman 2016).

He won his election pretty handily. In the 2016 Missouri gubernatorial election, Greitens beat his opponent by almost five points and by winning every county in the state save for four. Very quickly, though, this meteoric rise would be followed by just as rapid a fall.

In 2015, Greitens had begun a consensual extra-marital relationship with his hairdresser. Again, on its own, this is not necessarily a problem for anyone except the people involved. In this case, however, the woman involved accused him of sexual assault and blackmail. These are both criminal charges, and in February 2018, the city prosecutor in St. Louis charged Greitens with a felony (Watkins 2018).

Remember that the Missouri Legislature has mechanisms to investigate and punish elected officials separately from the criminal justice system? In this case, the Missouri House of Representatives formed a committee to investigate the claims that Greitens' relationship with his hairdresser was not as simple as two grown and consenting adults having an affair.

Around the same time, on April 20, 2018, the circuit court attorney charged him with a second felony, alleging that Greitens tampered with a computer at his veterans' aid charity and took email and donor lists in order to use them for political fundraising. Even though he founded the organization, it is illegal to use the lists for political purposes (Domonoske 2018).

On May 22, 2018, Missouri lawmakers opened a special session of the legislature, with the implication that their agenda could include impeachment proceedings against the governor. The felony invasion of privacy charges were dropped for lack of evidence; however, facing possible impeachment and the remaining criminal charges, Governor Greitens resigned from office on May 29, 2018 (Smith and Bosman 2018).

Discussion Questions

1. Is it ok that impeachment is largely a political tool rather than a legal one? Why or why not?
2. Does it surprise you that only 9 governors have ever been removed from office after an impeachment? Why or why not?
3. What kinds of misdeeds do you feel are bad enough to remove a governor from office?
4. Should it be harder or easier to remove a governor from office? Explain your answer.
5. Governors can be charged with crimes while holding office, but the President of the U.S. cannot. Which do you think is appropriate, and why?

Key Concepts

* Impeachment
* Resignation
* State Ethics Commissions
* Attorney General
* State Auditor

For More Information:

https://ballotpedia.org/Missouri_Impeachment_Process_Amendment_(2020)
https://law.justia.com/constitution/alabama/CA-245712.html
www.nga.org/consulting/powers-and-authority/

The Gubernatorial Incumbency Advantage

In 2018, 36 states held gubernatorial elections. In sixteen of these races, the incumbent was running for reelection. Guess how many of those incumbents was beaten by a challenger? Half? A quarter? Nope—only one. Scott Walker in Wisconsin was the only incumbent governor running for reelection in 2018 who lost the race.

This is not particularly unusual. In fact, since the 1950s, incumbents seeking reelection have held on to their seats over 70% of the time. Alaska is the only state in which incumbent governors have lost more bids for an additional term than they have won (Ostermeier 2018). It makes sense that incumbents would have an advantage over their challengers; they have some pretty serious advantages. They almost always have more name recognition than their opponent (Americans aren't great at knowing about their government but most can at least name their state's governor). Incumbents also tend to have better access to campaign finances as well as government resources that can indirectly be used to boost a campaign.

In order to counter this advantage and to ensure rotation in office, most states restrict the number of terms of office a governor may hold. This is often referred to as a term limit. Governors of 36 states are subject to term limits (Ballotpedia n.d.), almost all of which (excluding Wyoming, which passed theirs as a law) are codified in their state constitutions. These limits range from the most popular version, which is a limit of two consecutive terms where the governor becomes eligible again after sitting out a term, to Virginia's version, where the governor can only serve one term before having to sit out. Eight states have a lifetime maximum of two terms.

There are many arguments for and against term limits. It is pretty well established in political theory and philosophy that people, when given power, will eventually be corrupted by it. It is also pretty clear that the founding fathers believed wholeheartedly in this principle as they tried to build limits on power into the Constitution. Proponents of term limits for governors argue the same thing. Forcing turnover in elected positions prevents the official from becoming too entrenched in a system in which he or she can benefit his or herself at the expense of the common good. The governor would have less time in office to make commitments to lobbyists and other special interest groups that may not be in the interest of the public. Term limits also may encourage elected officials to remain closer to the daily realities of the American people rather than becoming removed and caught up in the weird world of politics and leadership.

On the other hand, career politicians who have devoted themselves to public service should be valued for their experience. It takes time to learn the administrative and political intricacies involved in managing the executive branch of an entire state. Why would we want to force a change just when someone is getting a feel for the job? Further, maybe term limits aren't even necessary. If a governor isn't doing a good job, the voters can simply vote for someone else. In fact, isn't it actually more democratic that way?

As it stands, most governors who run for reelection win. This is true in states where they can only be governor twice, and it is true in states where they can be governor as many times as the people of the state vote them in. So, what happened to Scott Walker?

He narrowly won races in 2010 and 2014. By many measures, he was a relatively successful governor for Wisconsin. When he took the job, the unemployment rate was over 9% and when he lost it was just under 3%. In the ten years prior to Walker's first term, college tuition in Wisconsin had doubled, but in the last eight years, it has remained frozen. When Walker moved into his Madison office in 2010, he had inherited a $3.6 billion budget shortfall, and now, even in the wake of some pretty hefty tax cuts, Wisconsin is running a budget surplus. Don't get me wrong, Walker did some things that weren't so popular too. Wisconsin has been a purple state for a long time, with roughly half of the population identifying as Democrats and the other half identifying as Republicans. Because of this split, Wisconsin had been pretty moderate politically until Walker took over. He took a sharp right on many issues. He rammed through legislation that took collective bargaining rights away from most public employee unions, sending their membership numbers crashing through the floor. He morphed Wisconsin into a right-to-work state for private-sector workers, hurting the unions even more. He substantially increased restrictions on abortion, imposed strict voter ID requirements, strengthened gun rights, and abolished civil service protections, a whole host of environmental regulations and tenure for professors in the University of Wisconsin system (Marley and Glauber 2019). At least a couple of those controversial actions were so unpopular that he had to stand for a recall election in 2012. And, as he noted himself shortly before the 2018 primary, there are still so many left-leaners in the state that the Democrats could put Daffy Duck on the ballot and still get 48% of the vote (Gilbert 2018).

So what happened? An incumbent governor presiding over a state that is doing well economically, where about half of the population should be a gimme in terms of their party affiliation—you would think that Walker should have had it in the bag. There was talk of a mythical "eight-year itch" in which voters get tired of an office-holder after two terms. And there was certainly evidence that Wisconsin voters acknowledge and support many of Walker's moves as governor but were getting antsy for even more movement in those areas. The budget was balanced, yes and that's great, but what about increasing teacher pay and fixing some of these roads and bridges? It is relatively easy for a challenger to find some priority that voters want further emphasized and promise all the things to all the people.

But if an eight-year itch is real, why is it that most governors who are eligible and run for a third term win? It seems more likely that other factors were at play in Walker's defeat. He has been a polarizing figure in Wisconsin for a long time. Many Wisconsinites are still sore about the 2011 Act 10 legislation that was so rough on unions and about his short-lived 2016 presidential run, which was widely panned by the people of Wisconsin as premature and ill-conceived.

Some feel that Walker's defeat had more to do with the President than with Walker's actual record as governor. Trump generally lacks support among independent voters in Wisconsin making it difficult for Walker to have wooed people to his team. And more specifically, Trump is deeply unpopular with some groups that had been key to Walker's previous victories—educated, white, suburban voters, and voters in the suburbs of Milwaukee. Walker had tried to walk a line, making public appearances with the president and being endorsed by him (Trump even referred to him as a "great friend"), but rarely referring to him on the campaign trail.

Considering Walker won by narrow margins in each of his previous elections and only narrowly avoided being recalled in 2012, it is perhaps not so surprising that while the American electorate remains so politically divided that a controversial governor in a divided state would have trouble. What remains to be seen is whether more incumbent governors will see the same difficulties moving forward.

Discussion Questions

1. There are term limits for governors in most states but not for members of U.S. Congress. Why?
2. There are pros and cons to term limits. Which do you find makes the better argument? Why?
3. Do you think running for president but not winning would hurt a governor back in their home state? Why or why not?
4. To what extent might having quick turnover of elected positions hurt a state?
5. To what extent might having quick turnover of elected positions benefit a state?

Key Terms

- Incumbency
- Reelection
- Term limits
- Recall election

For More Information:

http://governors.rutgers.edu/on-governors/us-governors/when-governors-seek-re-election/

www.sciencedirect.com/science/article/abs/pii/S0176268018302362

www.nytimes.com/2018/11/07/us/elections-wisconsin-governor-evers-walker.html

Can a State Make a Difference on Environmental Policy? California Is Giving It a Shot

In 2015, when world leaders met up in Paris to come up with an agreement on combatting climate change, then-California Governor Jerry Brown was there. He was worried that the political stalemate between President Obama and Congress was going to impede any chance the United States had to make real progress toward slowing climate change. And then, in 2017, new President Trump withdrew from the agreement completely. That, however, did not stop Governor Brown's own crusade. But how much impact can a state executive make when the federal government isn't on board?

Well, in the case of California, the answer is perhaps quite a bit. With a population of nearly 40 million people and a land mass bigger than all but two other states (United States Census Bureau 2018), California has the potential to be enormously influential. They boast a $3 trillion (yep, $3 trillion) gross state product (Wang and Aversa 2020). To put that in perspective, even though California is just one of 50 states, it makes up nearly a sixth of the entire nation's economy. The next biggest, Texas, sits at an impressive $1.8 trillion, but they really aren't even close. Way down at the other end of this list is Vermont with just $34 billion (and, of course, far fewer people). These kinds of numbers mean that if California were a country rather than a state, it would have the fifth largest economy in the world (even larger than India, France, and the UK).

California had long been the go-to example of terrible environmental quality. Have you seen any old movies or TV shows where the air is just sort of … brown? Well, that was Los Angeles. Even today, according to the American Lung Association, seven of the ten most polluted cities (American Lung Association 2018) in the U.S. are in California[1].

While it is true that California really struggles to maintain a clean and healthy state, it is also true that they have been at the forefront of aggressive environmental policy for a long time. Back in 1965, California was the first state to place limits on vehicle exhaust. A couple of years after that, they set the country's first air quality standards. These policies were a big deal and a huge step forward. Californians, especially Southern Californians, live in a much lower-density environment than, say, Manhattanites. This means that they drive. They drive everywhere. Adding to that, there is a substantial amount of truck traffic coming in and out of Mexico on a daily basis and the ports like the Port of Los Angeles also pile pollution on to the total. Even Congress recognized California's particular situation and voted to allow the state to enforce pollution standards that are more restrictive than those required at the federal level.

Air pollution has been the focus of California's environmental policy for a long time, but these days they have shifted to initiatives on climate change. In 2002, then Governor Gray Davis signed Assembly Bill 1493 over the loud and sustained protests of the auto industry. This was the first law that specifically addressed the greenhouse gasses that are emitted by automobiles. AB 1493 required that automakers would produce cars and light trucks that would emit 22% fewer greenhouse gasses by 2012 and 30% fewer by 2016 (PBS NOW 2005). The auto industry freaked out and tried to have the law overturned, but even the next governor, Arnold Schwarzenegger (a known lover of the Hummer), thought it was a good idea. In fact, thirteen more states decided to create their own version of the California standards. This meant that approximately 40% of the cars on American roads are covered by these more stringent rules. This is a high enough percentage that car manufacturers are designing their vehicles to meet these standards and selling them all over the country rather than having a California-standards version and a federal-standards version. Thus, California's environmental policy ended up driving technological change in the transportation industry nationally and internationally.

In 2009, President Obama announced that the federal government would adopt a fuel economy policy that would bring the federal standards in line with the California standards. In 2018, though, President Trump's administration announced plans to roll back the Obama-era tailpipe emissions regulations and to revoke California's permission to impose higher standards. Negotiations have been taking place ever since, but the leadership in California has pledged to continue to fight. It is interesting to note here that there is a bit of a bizarro-world thing going on here with regard to states' rights. Trump supporters are generally in favor of expansive states' rights and disdain federal interference into state business, while environmentalists usually sway toward supporting federal control over things like this. This, my friends, is what we refer to as "ad hoc" federalism (Smith and Greenblatt 2020).

It is without question that California has done more to advance the agenda on environmentalism than any other state. It would also be disingenuous to discount Governor Brown's role in all of it. In his sixteen years as governor (he retired after his non-consecutive fourth term in 2019), he had been known for taking measures to decrease the demand for coal and oil-based energy as well as for his leadership in getting other politicians on board, both nationally and internationally. He was able to get republican lawmakers on board to pass a cap-and-trade program, restricting greenhouse gas emissions while also allowing companies to buy and sell allowances to emit those same gasses. He set a lofty goal to have five million electric cars on the road by 2030, a number that California is on target to hit. He signed a law that would require 100% of California's electricity be carbon-free by 2045. He also leads The Climate Group in the Under2 Coalition in working with state and regional governments to keep global temperature from rising more than two degrees Celsius (Roberts 2018).

All of this doesn't mean that Governor Brown is universally applauded. Of course, those on the side of the automobile industry and President Trump criticize Brown's California for going too far. It is true that it costs more to build cars that hold up to the stricter pollution standards, and that is tough on the automakers. Brown also gets some flak from the environmentalists as well. Criticism from the left is generally related to Governor Brown's perceived support for oil production and fracking. The combination of plate tectonics, heat, and time melted the remains of prehistoric creatures into big pools of oil, and for the past century and a half, humans have been sucking it back out of the ground. California is home to some of the nation's biggest oil fields and, according to the American Petroleum Institute, produces more than half a billion barrels per day and supports nearly a million jobs. Brown defended himself against the criticism, saying that he can't just snap his fingers and make an entire industry disappear, and even if he was able to do that in California, the oil would just come from elsewhere.

Perhaps he has a point. Or maybe his critics do. Probably both. It does illustrate one of the problems with a state trying to tackle a problem like air pollution though. Even a giant, rich state like California is only one state. They can make a big difference, like they have with influencing how cars are built, but they may not have the ability to do it all.

Discussion Questions

1. In 2019, President Trump announced plans to prevent California from having higher standards than the federal ones. Should he be able to do that? Why or why not?
2. Do you think states can make a difference when it comes to things like environmental policy?
3. Do large states like California have an extra obligation to try to lead on topics such as this?

Key Terms

- Environmental policy
- Federalism
- Fuel standards
- Greenhouse gas emissions

For More Information:

https://en.wikisource.org/wiki/California_AB_1493
www.hoover.org/research/californias-green-governor-climate-hero-wrinkled-cape
www.under2coalition.org/

Note

1 Fun(ish) story. When I was younger and far more fun and reckless, I decided to go hang gliding off the side of a cliff just outside of Los Angeles. There was a short class, some safety videos, and finally they strapped me and the instructor, who would ostensibly keep me from dying, on to the glider. The last thing the instructor said to me before he flung me off the cliff was both interesting and terrifying. He told me to look at the smog line. It was a pretty clear line that day, blue sky above it and hazier greyish below. Apparently, in the LA area that is how you know how high you can go in the glider. The inversion forces that keep the smog below a certain level are the same forces that would keep our glider operating properly. Handy, I guess?

Works Cited

American Lung Association. (2018). *Most Polluted Cities, Then and Now*. https://www.lung.org/blog/sota-then-and-now

Ballotpedia. (n.d.). *Gubernatorial impeachment procedures*. Retrieved October 14, 2020, from https://ballotpedia.org/Gubernatorial_impeachment_procedures

Ballotpedia. (n.d.). *States with gubernatorial term limits*. Retrieved October 14, 2020, from https://ballotpedia.org/States_with_gubernatorial_term_limits

Blinder, A. (2017, April 10). Robert Bentley, Alabama Governor, Resigns Amid Scandal (Published 2017). *The New York Times*. https://www.nytimes.com/2017/04/10/us/robert-bentley-alabama-governor.html

Cooperman, J. (2016, April 14). *A Closer Look at Eric Greitens, Missouri's Governor-Elect*. Www.Stlmag.Com. https://www.stlmag.com/news/can-eric-greitens-become-missouri-s-next-governor/

Domonoske, C. (2018). *Missouri Governor Accused Of New Felony, After Allegations Of Assault And Blackmail*. NPR. https://www.npr.org/sections/thetwo-way/2018/04/18/603680224/missouri-governor-accused-of-new-felony-after-allegations-of-assault-and-blackma

Gilbert, C. (2018). *Gov. Scott Walker warns his GOP base that he may start out behind in the general election*. Milwaukee Journal Sentinel. https://www.jsonline.com/story/news/politics/elections/2018/08/13/scott-walker-warns-gop-base-he-may-start-out-behind-general-election/979795002/

Marley, P., & Glauber, B. (2019). *Scott Walker's eight years as governor ushered in profound change in Wisconsin*. Milwaukee Journal Sentinel. https://www.jsonline.com/story/news/politics/2019/01/04/scott-walkers-eight-years-wisconsin-governor-were-consequential/2473616002/

National Conference of State Legislators. (n.d.). Impeachment. www.ncsl.Org. Retrieved October 14, 2020, from https://www.ncsl.org/research/about-state-legislatures/impeachment.aspx

PBS NOW. (2005). *Science & Health. Air Wars - California's Auto Emissions Laws* https://www.pbs.org/now/science/caautoemissions2.html

Ostermeier, E. (2018, October 18). *In Which States Have Incumbent Governors Struggled to Win Reelection?* Smart Politics. https://editions.lib.umn.edu/smartpolitics/2018/10/18/in-which-states-have-incumbent-governors-struggled-to-win-reelection/

Roberts, D. (2018, September 11). *California Gov. Jerry Brown casually unveils history's most ambitious climate target*. Vox. https://www.vox.com/energy-and-environment/2018/9/11/17844896/california-jerry-brown-carbon-neutral-2045-climate-change

Smith, K. B., & Greenblatt, A. (2020). *Governing states and localities*. Sage | Cq Press.

Smith, M., & Bosman, J. (2018, May 29). Missouri's Governor, a Rising G.O.P. Star, Resigns Amid Scandal (Published 2018). *The New York Times*. https://www.nytimes.com/2018/05/29/us/eric-greitens-resigns.html

United States Census Bureau. (2018). *QuickFacts: California*. Census Bureau QuickFacts; United States Census Bureau. https://www.census.gov/quickfacts/ca

Wang, C., & Aversa, J. (2020). *Gross Domestic Product by State, 4th Quarter and Annual 2019*. https://www.bea.gov/system/files/2020-04/qgdpstate0420.pdf

Watkins, E. (2018). *Missouri Gov. Eric Greitens indicted*. CNN. https://www.cnn.com/2018/02/22/politics/missouri-eric-greitens/index.html

9

STATE COURT SYSTEMS

State and local courts play a profound role in their state governments. They resolve civil disputes and hand out justice in criminal cases. They also protect the citizens of their states from unconstitutional behavior by the political branches of government. Despite the importance of this role, or perhaps because of it, judicial systems differ tremendously from state to state. There are organizational differences from initial trial to final appeal. Judges in some states are elected by voters and in others are appointed by the governor. Such differences reflect each state's unique orientation toward the values of politics, law, judicial independence, and accountability.

This chapter looks at different aspects of the court system by looking at very different cases. The first, In Loco Parentis, analyzes how state courts have changed in terms of how they see the colleges and universities as being responsible for the well-being (and not just the education) of their students. Then, we talk about the justices themselves and the tension between allegiance to the law and allegiance to the wishes of constituents by examining the Brock Turner rape case in California. Finally, we move to a story about the relationship between a Native American Reservation in South Dakota and a town full of liquor stores in Nebraska and how the Nebraska State Supreme Court has handled the ensuing problems over the past several years.

In Loco Parentis

Before the fall semester in 1911, Berea College in Kentucky revised their student code. It had previously said that students were forbidden from entering "any place of ill repute, liquor saloons, gambling houses" or places similar. The revisions added a prohibition against students going to "eating houses and places of amusement" not controlled by the college. The punishment for going to a restaurant off campus? Expulsion (Lee 2011).

About two weeks before the beginning of that school year, J.S. Gott, a local businessman, bought a restaurant across the street from Berea College. This business had been there for a while and had thrived due to its proximity to the campus and its hungry students. Mr. Gott was not aware that Berea College was changing its rules, and when he found out, he was understandably upset. After all, he thought he was making a wise business decision, buying a restaurant next to a college. Plus, can a college even do that? Controlling what adults do outside of their campus?

Well, back in 1911, the answer was yes, colleges could do that. The court in Kentucky was sympathetic about Gott's lack of business, but ultimately they ruled Berea College was acting in loco parentis (Latin for "in the place of a parent") (Loss 2014). This term refers to the legal responsibility of a person or organization to take on some of the functions and responsibilities of a parent and historically has been seen as allowing institutions such as college to act in the best interests of the students as they see fit. And until the 1960s or so, it was common for colleges and universities to subject their students to restrictions on their private lives. Curfews were common (especially for women), students could be expelled for acting in "immoral" ways, restrictions on free speech and public demonstration were more common than not. As the Kentucky Supreme Court said,

> College authorities stand in loco parentis concerning the physical and moral welfare, and mental training of the pupils, and we are unable to see why to that end they may not make any rule or regulation for the government, or betterment of their pupils that a parent could for the same purpose. Whether the rules or regulations are wise, or their aims worthy, is a matter left solely to the discretion of the authorities, or parents as the case may be, and in the exercise of that discretion, the courts are not disposed to interfere, unless the rules and aims are unlawful, or against public policy.
>
> (Gott v. Berea College, 1913, p. 379)

Beginning in the 1960s, though, the idea that colleges and universities were acting in place of their students' parents and could exercise that level of control started to wane. Prior to this, the courts had allowed colleges to do things like expel students, without any version of due process, for pretty much anything, like having "offensive habits" at Stetson University in Florida in 1924 (Stetson v. Hunt 1924) or for being bad for the "moral atmosphere" like at Syracuse in 1928 (Anthony v. Syracuse University 1928). In 1960, Alabama State College expelled a group of black students who, after having been refused service at a lunch counter at the Montgomery County Courthouse, participated in a civil rights protest. Alabama State College expelled the students without any due process. They were not given the chance to defend themselves or to appeal the decision. The students sued the school for violating their constitutional right to due process (Katz 2018).

This time the case was heard in federal court, the Fifth Circuit Court to be specific, and the justices decided that students at tax-supported schools should be given due process protections before facing expulsion or other major disciplinary actions. Remember that even though the U.S. Constitution's guarantee of these rights were originally interpreted as meaning that the federal government had to abide by them, the Fourteenth Amendment made it so that states had to ensure the same rights as well. So, the court said that students have the right to:

- Be given notice of the charges against them/grounds for punishment;
- Have access to the names of witnesses against them and the facts that the witnesses will testify about;
- The chance to defeat themselves against the charges and the testimony of the witnesses;
- An opportunity to review the results and findings of hearings in the matter.

The civil rights era brought about several similar cases, all around the country and a legal precedent emerged: public colleges and universities[1] are NOT acting in loco parentis and cannot impose the kinds of strict rules and punishments on students that they had in the past. One of the consequences of this was that these schools were no longer held responsible when something bad happened to their students. For example, in 1979, a student at California Polytechnic State University was severely injured in a car crash that was the result of a drunken race. She sued the school, alleging that they had a duty to protect her from dangerous situations that violated the student code of conduct. The California court system disagreed. They held that if students were going to be given the independence and rights of adults (and remember too, that in 1971 the voting age changed from 21 to 18), that their school didn't have the responsibility of protecting them in cases like these (Bendlin 2015). A few years later, in 1986, the Utah Supreme Court agreed in a similar case. A University of Utah student was injured falling off of a cliff on a school-sponsored field trip. The student, who was underage, had been drinking alcohol prior to the fall and subsequently sued the university for not protecting her (Beach v. University of Utah). The court ruled in favor of the University, saying that colleges and universities are educational facilities, not custodial ones. The new theme became, "if students are adults, they have to take on the responsibilities of adults."

This doesn't mean that schools get to completely abandon all responsibility for the safety of their students. The Delaware Supreme Court ruled on a case in 1991 where a student was severely burned during a fraternity hazing incident, saying that the University has a duty to regulate and supervise foreseeable dangerous activities on its property (Furek v. University of Delaware). Further, many schools have voluntarily taken it upon themselves to commit to the safety of their students, even if it falls short of the old in loco parentis standards. In 1997, a student at Colgate University fell from a fraternity house balcony and sued the university. In line with the modern standards, the courts in New York ruled that Colgate was not responsible (Rothbard v. Colgate University). Colgate, however, decided to take it upon itself to proactively make its campus a safer place for its students, creating programs to educate students on the dangers of irresponsible alcohol use, providing students with increased social opportunities that are alcohol-free, and providing increased support for safe transportation, emergency phones, and community-based living arrangements.

Discussion Questions

1. Do you feel like your school should be responsible for your actions off campus? Are there limits?
2. How does the changing understanding of how the human brain develops between the ages of 18–22 affect how we see the role of colleges and universities?
3. If a student wanted to start a club for Nazi sympathizers, should a school let them because of free speech or do they have a responsibility to protect the other students who might be hurt by the group?
4. Should a school be held responsible for the actions of sororities and fraternities on their campus? What if the houses are off campus?

Key Terms

- In loco parentis
- Due process
- Fourteenth Amendment

For More Information:

www.insidehighered.com/blogs/higher-ed-gamma/reimagining-loco-parentis
https://law.justia.com/cases/federal/district-courts/FSupp/186/945/2374127/
https://nebhe.org/journal/support-responsibilities-in-an-age-of-campus-suicide/

Judicial Recall: How the Brock Turner Case Turned California on Its Head

On January 18, 2015, two Swedish students at Stanford University were walking on campus when they came up upon a disturbing scene. Brock Turner, a student athlete at the University, was sexually assaulting an unconscious woman behind a garbage dumpster. Turner attempted to flee, so the two apprehended and restrained him until the police arrived and took Turner into custody. Turner was arrested and charged with two counts of rape, two counts of felony sexual assault, and one count of attempted rape.

The rape charges were eventually dropped, but the trial on the other charges began in March 2016. Turner was convicted of the three remaining charges of felony sexual assault. He faced a potential sentence of fourteen years in prison. On June 2, 2016, Santa Clara County Superior Court Judge Aaron Persky delivered a surprising sentence. Turner was to serve a term of six months in the Santa Clara County Jail (he had already done half of this) and a three-year period of probation (Svrluga 2016).

The outcome of the case shocked many people. It seemed like such a light punishment for a pretty terrible crime. As a result, the California legislature changed the laws so that there would be a required prison term (mandatory minimum) for people convicted of sexual assault and so that digital penetration would be included in the state's definition of rape. This in itself was a huge change, but a more surprising change was about to happen. By January 24, 2018, the Santa Clara County Registrar of Voters certified that a petition to recall Judge Persky from office had gained enough signatures to have the measure put on the ballot. It would be the first time a judge in California had been recalled in 86 years (Astor, 2018).

Just like different states have different ways of selecting judges, states handle the removal of judges differently. Most states have a mechanism by which judges can be impeached by the state legislature. Some states allow the state supreme court to remove a judge. Some states give the governor the authority to remove judges (though it is generally not as simple as the governor just deciding to remove someone). In ten states (Arizona, California, Colorado, Georgia, Minnesota, Montana, Nevada, North Dakota, Oregon, and Wisconsin), judges can be recalled by the voters. This process varies a bit, but generally requires a certain number of signatures on a petition. Once the petition is certified as having enough signatures, the question of whether to recall the judge goes on the ballot, either during the next election or as a special election. Voters then decide whether or not to keep the judge (Ballotpedia n.d.). And in Judge Persky's case, by a 60-40 margin, voters decided not to keep him.

While many victim advocate groups and women's groups hailed Judge Persky's ouster as a victory, legal experts aren't so sure. Judge Persky didn't commit any act of misconduct or anything illegal. His record on the bench was a strong one. He had no history of accusations of unfair sentences or favoring certain types of defendants. Whether or not you agree that Brock Turner's sentence was too light (and lots of lawyers, judges, and probation/corrections experts have chimed in, many of whom think Persky's judgement was reasonable) (Brown 2016), it is worth considering the implications of a system where a judge, who should ostensibly be concerned with the law and legal precedent rather than politics and popularity, can be removed for doing something unpopular.

Let's take a mental journey back to the 1950s. The ruling Brown v. Board reversed previous rulings and found that school segregation was unconstitutional. In many parts of the country, this was a deeply unpopular ruling. Even President Eisenhower expressed disappointment in Chief Justice Earl Warren's decision and his part in making it happen (Eisenhower had been the one to appoint Warren) (Fassuliotis 2019). If the Supreme Court justices or the federal court judges who were charged with handling Brown's implementation had been subject to recall based on the public's emotional reaction to school desegregation … well, we might still have some states with officially segregated schools.

The idea behind the ability of a citizenry to recall elected officials is to increase accountability. It is a more pure form of democracy, even. One might argue that the downsides of judicial recalls outweigh the good though. Judges know that voters generally prefer harsher punishments for people convicted of a crime. For all of the talk about the overwhelming numbers of drug offenders choking up the justice system, only around 15% of convicted criminals fall into this category (Sawyer and Wagner 2020). The majority of people serving time in state prison are there for violent crimes. No justice who is up for reelection or facing a recall wants to be seen as soft on crime, and studies show that judges tend to impose harsher sentences right before election season. The potential for making the public unhappy has a significant influence on sentencing.

Getting rid of judicial elections or public recall mechanisms would not necessarily mean a loss of accountability. Also, remember that 40 states don't use this procedure anyway. Judges can be removed by other means, namely impeachment by the state legislature or, upon the advice of a judicial ethics council (in most cases), removal by the state supreme court. If judges are concerned that unpopular rulings in difficult cases might get them booted from the bench, perhaps it is worth considering that removals shouldn't happen by the whim of public emotion, but by those who are more carefully trained in law and public policy and who have more experience in the context of the cases that the judges see.

Discussion Questions

1. What are the benefits of being able to recall a judge? What are the drawbacks?
2. Should there be a higher threshold for recalling a judge than not agreeing with a decision they made?
3. How involved should legal experts be in the hiring and firing of judges?
4. This situation brings up the tension between democracy and expertise. How should Americans balance these two concepts?

Key Terms

- Recall election
- Mandatory minimum
- Judicial selection/removal
- Accountability

For More Information

www.ncsl.org/research/elections-and-campaigns/recall-of-state-officials.aspx
https://ballotpedia.org/Laws_governing_recall
www.brennancenter.org/sites/default/files/publications/How_Judicial_Elections_Impact_Criminal_Cases.pdf

Selling Beer to Alcoholics: The Nebraska State Supreme Court and the Whiteclay Problem

Whiteclay, Nebraska is so tiny and so remote that it doesn't appear on many maps. The population hovers around ten, and though the unincorporated area is inside the boundaries of Nebraska, it is far more closely associated with an area just to its north in South Dakota: the Pine Ridge Indian Reservation. This association is so strong that even the 2000 Census erroneously called Whiteclay, "Pine Ridge."

Unlike many of the rural areas in northern Nebraska, Whiteclay has been prosperous. The median income in 2000 was $76,250 per family. Not a single family or individual was listed as falling below the poverty line. Compare this to the larger (890 people) Rushville, Nebraska located about 20 miles south. The median income for a family in Rushville during the same time period was $36,100. 16.4% of the population of Rushville is below the poverty line (Wikipedia 2012).

Much of the relative prosperity in Whiteclay can be attributed to one thing—beer. Until 2017, Whiteclay (and all ten of its residents) hosted four liquor stores. In 2010, beer sales at these four stores totaled almost 5 million cans (about 13,000 cans per day) for a mind-boggling $3 million in gross sales. These numbers may not make much sense, until you remember that not quite two miles north of Whiteclay sits a giant Indian Reservation that is home to 40,000 people and does not allow any alcohol sales on its property.

Alcoholism is a real problem within Native communities and it is no joke in Pine Ridge. As many as 2/3 of the adults living on the reservation are alcoholics and approximately a quarter of the children are born with fetal alcohol syndrome. These struggles are why the Oglala Lakota Sioux banned all alcohol sales from the reservation but also why Whiteclay liquor store owners have been able to thrive for the past hundred-plus years. According to Mary Frances Berry of the U.S. Commission on Civil Rights, Whiteclay can be said to exist only to sell beer to the Oglala Lakota (Laughland and Silverstone, 2019).

13,000 cans of beer a day, but the customers aren't supposed to take it home to drink it, and there are no bars or other publicly-accessible options to hang out in Whiteclay to drink it. More than 1,000 citations for driving under the influence had been issued annually on the two-mile stretch between Whiteclay and Pine Ridge. Public drunkenness and violence in Whiteclay itself and the severe alcoholism problems on the Reservation have been problems for a very long time, but more recently the activism to end alcohol sales ramped up.

In 1999, a pair of unsolved murders of Lakota men focused activist attention on the Whiteclay/Pine Ridge alcohol problem and groups ranging from the American Indian Movement to Nebraskans for Peace asked that Nebraska revoke the liquor licenses that were allowing the four stores to supply the Reservation. After all, not only does federal law prohibit the sale and distribution of alcohol on reservations unless explicitly allowed by the tribal government, the state also has the right to regulate alcohol sales that contribute to unruliness and lawbreaking (just like how a bar that keeps getting in trouble for serving minors can lose its liquor license).

The Oglala Lakota Sioux Tribe filed a federal lawsuit in 2012 against the liquor stores and against some of the major beer companies alleging that they knowingly sold beer to be consumed on the Reservation (Abourezk 2012). The judge in the case dismissed the suit saying that it wasn't a federal issue and should be handled on the state level. The Nebraska Legislature kicked around some policy ideas, including limiting sales hours or ban the sale of certain products in a proposed "alcohol impact zone," but no real changes were made. That is, until 2017 when the Nebraska Liquor Control Commission denied the applications from the four stores to renew their liquor licenses. Suddenly, the plentiful and convenient supply of beer to Pine Ridge had been cut off.

Unsurprisingly, the liquor store owners freaked out and appealed the decision. This was their livelihood, after all. But the Liquor Commission held the line. The biggest problem, from their point of view, was the lack of proper law enforcement. Whiteclay, they noted, has no town government or police force. The closest Sheriff Department is almost 30 miles away. By law, they held, adequate law enforcement is a necessary condition for the issuance of a liquor license, and the lack thereof in Whiteclay is a substantial threat to public health and safety.

Attorneys for the liquor store owners pushed back. The stores have been legal businesses, with no substantial changes for many years. One of the store's owner has held the license since 1982. All of a sudden there isn't enough law enforcement? And what about other rural areas that don't have a police force? Are they going to lose their licenses too? A District Court judge agreed, siding with the businesses and voiding the Alcohol Commission's decision. The disagreements continued and the Nebraska Attorney General took the case to the Nebraska Supreme Court.

The Nebraska Supreme Court isn't there to decide whether it is right to sell beer to alcoholics. It isn't even there to decide whether there is enough law enforcement around Whiteclay to justify a liquor license. It is there to focus on legal procedure and jurisdictional issues. This means that the court was really only going to look at whether the Commission had the authority to make the decision that they did and whether their process and the processes of the lower court were handled appropriately. So, on one side, you have the Attorney General arguing that the Liquor Control Commission gets the final say on licensure issues, and on the other side, you have the store owners who were arguing that the District Court Judge had the authority to overturn the commission's decision. Is this executive branch/administrative territory or is it up to the courts?

After all of this drama—copious amounts of beer, violence, alcoholism, drunk driving, store owners being stripped of their ability to conduct business—the Nebraska Supreme Court's decision came down to a procedural technicality. When the attorney for the liquor stores filed their initial lawsuit in the District Court, they named the Liquor Control Commission and the Attorney General in the complaint. They had not included, however, the Nebraska residents who had made the complaints of the public safety issues. The Supreme Court held that these individuals were party to the proceedings and should have been part of the appeal. The result was that the District Court ruling was invalid and the Commission's denial of the license renewal was to stand (Hammel 2017).

It has been a little more than three years since alcohol has been sold in Whiteclay, and the problems didn't just disappear. Social and public health issues such as these are not so easy to just solve, and frankly, it wasn't the Supreme Court's job to solve the problem. Though big questions of human and civil rights are often decided by these high courts, the bulk of what they do is extremely technical and procedural. Though the attorney who won his case lauded the decision as one that helped a "shameful chapter in Nebraska history come to a close," it is certainly possible that a similar situation will pop up either in Whiteclay or a similar border area. After all, drawing an income that is more than twice the local average is likely pretty tempting.

Discussion Questions

1. To what extent is the government's responsibility to keep people from harming themselves?
2. In what ways do problems like alcohol and drugs harm society and not just the individual?
3. Do Americans have a particular responsibility to Native communities because of harm done in the past? Why or why not?

Key Terms

- Median Income
- Liquor Control Commission
- Attorney General
- Reservations

For More Information

www.omaha.com/news/state_and_regional/dry-for-a-year-whiteclay-has-cleaned-up-but-some/article_ccf057c7-d9f1-5661-aaad-23b8ccd15b74.html
https://apnews.com/3ee73175ddf3498c9c8e9233c0c7d4bb
https://pubs.niaaa.nih.gov/publications/arh22-4/253.pdf

Note

1 Private colleges and universities are a whole different thing all together. Because they aren't tax-funded or governed by a public entity, they have far more leeway to obligate contractual relationships between themselves and their students that require adherence to rules and acceptance of potential consequences. This doesn't mean that all of your Constitutionally-protected rights go out the door as soon as you enroll as a private college student, but it is far more complicated and the legal precedent is different.

Works Cited

Anthony v. Syracuse University, (NY App Div 1928)

Abourezk, K. (2012). *Oglala Sioux Tribe sues Whiteclay stores, beer makers, distributors*. Lincoln Journal Star. https://journalstar.com/news/local/oglala-sioux-tribe-sues-whiteclay-stores-beer-makers-distributors/article_d093add7-c3e6-5ae2-86a1-e12785c1f063.html

Astor, M. (2018, June 6). California Voters Remove Judge Aaron Persky, Who Gave a 6-Month Sentence for Sexual Assault. *The New York Times*. https://www.nytimes.com/2018/06/06/us/politics/judge-persky-brock-turner-recall.html

Ballotpedia. (n.d.). *Laws governing recall*. Retrieved October 19, 2020, from https://ballotpedia.org/Laws_governing_recall

Beach v. University of Utah, (Supreme Court of Utah 1986)

Bendlin, S. (2015). *Cocktails on Campus: Are Libations a Liability? Cocktails on Campus: Are Libations a Liability?* Barry University School of Law. https://lawpublications.barry.edu/cgi/viewcontent.cgi?article=1056&context=facultyscholarship

Brown, D. (2016). *Judge in Brock Turner Sexual Assault Case Cleared of Misconduct After Weak Sentencing.* Www.Vice.Com. https://www.vice.com/en/article/yp87w5/judge-in-brock-turner-sexual-assault-case-cleared-of-misconduct-after-weak-sentencing

Fassuliotis, W. (2019). *Ike's Mistake: The Accidental Creation of the Warren Court.* Virginia Law Weekly. https://www.lawweekly.org/col/2018/10/17/ikes-mistake-the-accidental-creation-of-the-warren-court

Furek v. University of Delaware, (Delaware Supreme Court 1991).

Hammel, P. (2017). *Supreme Court delivers victory to opponents of Whiteclay beer sales; "The shame of Whiteclay is over," attorney says.* Omaha World Herald. https://omaha.com/state-and-regional/supreme-court-delivers-victory-to-opponents-of-whiteclay-beer-sales-the-shame-of-whiteclay-is/article_653a39aa-a51b-11e7-9823-ef5e85336ab8.html

John, B. Stetson University v. Hunt, (Florida 1924).

Katz, B. (2018). *58 Years Later, Alabama Clears the Records of 29 Black Students Who Protested Segregation.* Smithsonian Magazine. https://www.smithsonianmag.com/smart-news/58-years-later-alabama-clears-records-29-black-students-who-protested-segregation-180969220/

Laughland, O., & Silverstone, T. (2019, February 19). *Liquid genocide: alcohol destroyed Pine Ridge reservation – then they fought back.* The Guardian; The Guardian. https://www.theguardian.com/society/2017/sep/29/pine-ridge-indian-reservation-south-dakota

Lee, P. (2011). *The Curious Life of In Loco Parentis at American Universities.* https://scholar.harvard.edu/files/philip_lee/files/vol8lee.pdf

Loss, C. P. (2014). Institutionalizing in Loco Parentis after Gott v. Berea College (1913). *Teachers College Record, 116*(12). https://eric.ed.gov/?id=EJ1044671

Rothbard v. Colgate University, (Supreme Court of New York 1997).

Sawyer, W., & Wagner, P. (2020, March 24). *Mass Incarceration: The Whole Pie 2020.* Www.Prisonpolicy.Org. https://www.prisonpolicy.org/reports/pie2020.html

Svrluga, S. (2016). 'I take him at his word': Judge in Stanford sexual assault case explained controversial sentence. *Washington Post.* https://www.washingtonpost.com/news/grade-point/wp/2016/06/14/i-take-him-at-his-word-judge-in-stanford-sexual-assault-case-explained-controversial-sentence/

Wikipedia. *Whiteclay.* (2012, August 30). https://en.wikipedia.org/wiki/Whiteclay

10

THE BUREAUCRACY

Bureaucracy is the public agencies and the public programs and services that these agencies implement and manage. Thus, bureaucrats are simply the employees of the public agencies. These agencies, generically known as government bureaucracies, usually are located in the executive branches of state and local governments. Although these agencies are very different in terms of the programs and services they manage and deliver, the vast majority of them are organizationally very similar.

Bureaucracy is often despised and disparaged. It is also clear that government bureaucracy is underestimated and does not get the credit it actually deserves. A wide range of state and local agencies support and deliver the programs and services that make up our social and economic life as we know it. Unfortunately, many young people never even consider working for government as a viable career option. The first section of this chapter spends time looking at the reasons for this and some opportunities to change it. We move right into some deeper discussion of this anti-bureaucracy attitude by looking at how people talk about the government workers in the U.S. and some of the implications of this line of rhetoric. Finally, we look at one of the functions of bureaucracy, regulation. It isn't a super popular thing to talk about in many circles, but this section gives an example, amusement park rides, that may give you a different perspective on the importance of government regulations.

Interesting Work, Good Benefits, and Job Security: Why Work for the Government?

Let's be honest, when most people picture working for the government, they don't picture anything very exciting. Pushing papers around under florescent lights, fighting against red tape to try and make do with low budgets and under-appreciative clients. Don't get me wrong—this exists. Of course, this exists. It also exists in many private businesses. But government work has developed a bit of a stigma over the years. A combination of a lack of trust in government itself combined with a culture that glamorizes Bay-area startups has led to a situation where a significant number of government workers are older than those in the private world. And considering how many public employees are eligible to retire within the next couple of years, all of the levels of government are facing a situation where they need to start really emphasizing recruitment from the younger population.

But young people don't seem to want to work for the government. The percentage of public employees under age 30 has been steadily decreasing for years and is significantly lower than in the private-sector workforce. And in our increasingly digital world, it is only going to get more and more important for government agencies to recruit and hire younger workers, even if it means that they need to rethink some of their structuring and recruiting.

With all of this said, government service offers features that should appeal to young workers. Michigan State University did a study where they gave a list of fifteen job characteristics to over 9,000 adults between the ages of eighteen and 25 (Chao and Gardner n.d.). The options were:

Good benefits
High income
Annual vacations
Interesting work
Travel opportunities
Limited stress
Chance for promotion
Job security
Opportunity to learn new skills
Geographical location
Flexible hours
Ability to work independently
Regular hours
Limited overtime
Regular hours

They found that the most important things that young people were looking for in a job are:

Interesting work
Good benefits
Job security

Chance for promotion
Opportunity to learn new skills
Location

While it is true that at most levels of employment, government employees don't make quite as much as their counterparts in the private sector, it turns out that young people aren't the money-grubbing little greed-monsters that some stereotypes say anyway. And when you look at the list of the characteristics that actually are the most important to young people, government work actually can fit the bill.

Let's start from the bottom. Location? Well, in addition to the 2,738,000 federal government jobs in the U.S.[1], there are approximately 2,446,300 state government jobs and around 14,165,000 local government jobs. Considering how the federal system of government works, with its layers of government entities, pretty much everywhere you go in the U.S. has some version of government work. You want to live in Hawaii? The day I wrote this, there were almost 300 available jobs listed on the state website and nearly 600 available federal jobs located in Hawaii. More interested in sticking closer to home? One of my favorite students is from Creston, Iowa in the rural southern part of the state. If she wanted to work within a 90-minute drive from her parents so she could visit often and eat their food, she could consider any of the more than 400 federal jobs located within this radius, the sixteen state jobs, or the two jobs currently available with the city of Creston itself (and of course all of the surrounding towns have their own job listings). I didn't even look at the county level or at any special districts like water or school districts that would be sure to add more to these numbers.

Now I'm going to combine a couple of these, interesting work and opportunity to learn new skills. What is it that you care about? Is there a problem that you want to solve or a topic that you are interested in? Government work can offer an opportunity to do so. If you care about education, security, homelessness, voting, or almost anything, you can find a government entity that focuses on that or work for an elected or appointed official that shares your vision. And because government agencies, especially at the state and local levels, do not tend to be super highly staffed, it is likely that your job responsibilities and opportunities will include a wide variety of things. Work for your state's Department of Labor? You may find yourself conducting an inspection of a construction site one day and assisting a single mother in collecting the back pay she is owed the next. See yourself as a Leslie Knope at your local Parks and Rec? During the warmer months you may oversee the maintenance of ball fields and t-ball leagues, while in the winter you may spend your time developing a proposal to build a new splash park.

Now, while you are doing these things, you are probably not going to get a catered lunch every day or a ping pong table, but in general, government jobs come with significant job security and the opportunity to move up. In the

U.S., over a third of state and local government workers and a quarter of federal government employees are members of a union (as opposed to 6.5% of private-sector workers) (Bureau of Labor Statistics 2020a). Unions help increase job stability (as well as pay and benefits), by insisting that employers conduct due process before an employee is terminated. And you don't have to be a member of the union to receive this benefit.[2] Job stability is helped further by the very fact that demand for government services is not decreasing. And when there are decreases in staffing, it is generally done through attrition—not replacing people when they leave or retire. You get a government job and if you do well and want to, you get to stay at that job. And because of the aging workforce that we discussed earlier, there are increasing opportunities to be promoted once you are in. You may start as a program assistant and end up being promoted to program manager pretty quickly if that manager becomes the director when that person retires.

Finally, benefits are one of the areas where people actually give public service some credit. Are public employees getting bonuses or stock buy-in opportunities, or snack carts? No, not usually. But do they get things like professional development, assistance with paying for graduate school, access to medical and fitness facilities, and financial counseling at higher rates that their private-sector peers? Yep. And of course, there is also the fact that almost all full-time public employees get health insurance and a retirement plan. In 2017, about 47% of private-sector employers offered health benefits, while 99% of full-time state employees receive them (Bureau of Labor Statistics 2020b).

Maybe it is time to rethink working for the government.

Discussion Questions

1. How would you rank the options given in the MSU survey? Why?
2. Why do you think that people's values and preferences for job characteristics change over time and across generations?
3. How can government agencies more effectively recruit younger employees?

Key Terms

- Bureaucracy
- Employment

For More Information:

http://cepr.net/documents/publications/benefits-state-local-2010-04.pdf
www.census.gov/programs-surveys/apes.html
http://ceri.msu.edu/publications/pdf/JobChar4-16.pdf

Bureaucrat Bashing in the Era of Civil Service Shame

In June of 1995, not quite two months after the terrorist bombing of the Oklahoma City Federal building, the New York Times published a letter to the editor from Mel Dubnick, a professor at Rutgers University in New Jersey (Dubnick 1995). The crux of the letter was that although those who work with and study the civil service know that those workers are hardworking, though overburdened and underappreciated, there is a dangerous myth floating around about bureaucrats and that the Times was contributing to it. Dubnick writes:

> The American public, with a good deal of help from politicians and the media, has made the Federal bureaucracy the scapegoat for many of our social, economic, and personal woes. Pundits of every type have made careers by perpetuating stereotypes and falsehoods built on myths of a growing bureaucratic Leviathan that pathologically abuses its power. In its bowels reside individuals variously characterized as incompetent, inept and even evil.

Bureaucracy, which is basically just a hierarchical institution that is run by rules and regulations, division of labor, and meritorious job positioning, can be used to talk about the public sector or the private one. Max Weber was the first to formally define and study bureaucracy the 1920s, arguing that it was pretty clearly the best way to organize large-scale human activity. This isn't to say that he liked it. Weber was concerned that a powerful bureaucratic machine was a threat to creativity and individual freedom.

Bureaucracy isn't supposed to be a pejorative term. It is what it is, a word that refers to a type of organizational structure and management, but it has taken on a pretty significant stigma, so much so that just saying the word causes many people to make a face. If you ask people what it is that is so very terrible about bureaucracy, it is likely that the answer will fall into one of two categories: it doesn't work as well as the private model or that it is discriminatory and biased.

In 1944, Ludwick Von Mises, an economist out of New York University, wrote a book called Bureaucracy (Von Mises 1944). In his book, he compared government bureaucracy with for-profit enterprise, and in his framework, bureaucracy doesn't come out looking good. He argued that because government bureaucracy is limited by laws and budgets, workers are chained to stagnant processes and have no room for creativity and problem-solving. Basically, there is no incentive to change or improve anything. This line of thinking has continued to this day. Enthusiasm for making government run more like a business was renewed in the mid-1990s after David Osborne and Ted Gaebler published their book, Reinventing Government (Osborne and Gaebler 1994). The New Public Management era was born and even Vice President Al Gore got on board when putting together the National Performance Review.

Those who subscribe to this thinking tend toward a singular solution: run government more like a business. As Osborne and Gaebler put it, government should focus more on the "steering" of policy and leave the "rowing", or delivery of services, to private enterprises that compete for the contracts. A turn toward market-oriented government, with an emphasis on competition, would lean on tools like franchises, vouchers, and the complete privatization of some services would, in their minds, lead to increased government efficiency and cost savings.

Bureaucracy is also criticized by many for being so rules-oriented and impersonal that it becomes oppressive and unfeeling toward the human beings that it is supposed to serve. In a 1940 article, "Bureaucratic Structure and Personality" (Merton 1940), Columbia University sociologist Robert K. Merton laid out the foundations of this critique. For Merton, the problem is that a system that is built around the idea that rigid rules and procedures and a system that rewards employees who follow these rules and procedures for as long as possible leads to those employees valuing the rules and procedures themselves more than the clients receiving the service.

Another sociologist (and economist), Thorstein Veblen termed this phenomenon "trained incapacity" (Wais 2005), meaning that doing the same thing over and over and over due to a strict procedure leads those employees to be unable to adapt for changing circumstances. Think of an employee at a DMV somewhere in rural Middle America. That employee knows how to process driver's licenses, right? Collect the application paperwork and the payment, make sure the test has been passed, determine the age and restrictions of the applicant, take the picture (make sure the face is clearly visible), print the receipt, and send the person on their way. No biggie, they do it every day of their working life. At this point in history, most states have rules that deal with various religious needs like veils and the like, but what happens then when that DMV employee has a customer come in with a face full of temporary tattoos? Is that considered having your face covered and you can't get your license with them? How would the employee even determine that they are temporary? Or what if a man is dressed in elaborate drag, including a wig and lots of makeup and false eyelashes? Isn't the point to be able to match the picture with the person for safety and bad-guy-catching reasons?

40 years after, Merton's paper discussed these problems. Michael Lipsky, who was a political scientist at MIT at the time, wrote a book called Street-Level Bureaucracy (Lipsky 2010). He also criticized the rigid nature of the bureaucratic machine, but focused on how the front-line workers like teachers, police officers, and yes, DMV employees, actually go about getting around the rigidity in order to do their jobs. Sure, every street-level bureaucrat should treat each and every client the same and according to the established rules and procedures, but in real life, these workers are over-committed and underfunded. In order to get by under these circumstances, they apply the rules slightly differently. Services are rationed or made harder to get; resources are kept scarce and wait lists long;

secretaries screen out difficult cases; applications are kicked back for tiny mistakes; services are stigmatized to discourage new applicants.

You can see evidence of Lipsky's ideas in the news. For instance, in 2013, Maryland received public criticism when it was discovered that they were excluding most of their special education and ESL students from standardized testing (Layton 2013). Maryland has often been ranked in the top spot on lists of states with excellent education, so when these numbers were brought to light, it led some to wonder if they were gaming the system. There is nothing TECHNICALLY illegal about what they did; in Maryland, it is up to the school to decide which special education and ESL students should take the test and other states exclude or exempt some students from the test as well. Maryland's rate though, excluding more than 60% of their students with disabilities is far far higher than the national average of 16%. Lipsky's framework applies here; the rules and procedures are important, as are the scores that determine how well the schools are doing. Thus, the rules are applied in a certain way as to make the system appear more successful.

Criticisms of the government bureaucracy are real and it is important in a democratic system that we look at our institutions with a critical eye; however, bashing on the civil service has gotten beyond healthy criticism in some circles. Presidential campaigns on both sides, but particularly for Republicans, have become a race to see who will claim to cut the most government employees. For instance, Ronald Reagan famously referred to the federal government as an "evil empire" (Reagan 1983) and said that the "most terrifying words in the English language are: I'm from the government and I'm here to help" (Reagan 1986). More recently in a now-infamous gaffe, Texas Governor Rick Perry was asked which three federal agencies he would cut if he became president, and he managed to only remember two of them but swore there was a third that he would get rid of even if he couldn't think of it at the moment (MacAskill 2011).

This kind of derision has consequences. A 2006 study for the Public Administration Review, "Assessing the Impact of Bureaucracy Bashing by Electoral Campaigns," conducted focus groups on public employees and found that all of the bashing and negative connotations surrounding the public service workforce left the workers with low morale, frustration and hostility, and the inability to work effectively with many elected officials. Further, the negative rhetoric has made it more difficult for agencies to recruit new workers, meaning that many of the public agencies around the country are facing a staffing crisis as their older employees retire without younger applicants to replace them.

There are more than 20 million public employees in the United States. Most of them work for your local governments providing utilities, teaching children, and keeping your towns and cities safe. Are they all awesome, civic-minded, soft-hearted superheroes? Nope. But perhaps historian and author Ian Morris put it best when he wrote that the words scarier than Reagans are, "There is no government and I'm here to kill you" (Morris 2014).

Discussion Questions

1. What does the word "bureaucracy" mean to you? What kind of images does it bring up?
2. Do you agree with Max Weber that there probably is one best way to organize large numbers of people? Is bureaucracy our only real option?
3. Is there some way we could go about changing the public perception of the bureaucracy? What might we try?

Key Terms

- Bureaucracy
- Management
- New Public Management
- Trained incapacity
- Street-level bureaucrats

For More Information:

https://onlinelibrary.wiley.com/doi/pdf/10.1111/j.1540-6210.2006.00575.x
www.politico.com/agenda/story/2017/09/27/aging-government-workforce-analysis-000525
www.nytimes.com/1995/06/15/opinion/1-bureaucrat-bashing-can-lead-to-tragedy-333295.html

Verruckt and the Case for Increased Government Regulation of Amusement Parks

On August 7, 2016, Caleb, the 10-year-old son of Kansas state representative Scott Schwab, was killed on a waterslide at the Schlitterbahn waterpark in Kansas City. The death occurred on the slide called Verruckt, the German word for insane, which at over 168 feet tall was touted as the world's tallest and where riders reached speeds up to 70 miles per hour, dropping at a mind-boggling 60-degree angle.

Amusement parks starting popping up around the U.S. in the late 19th century following the invention of the first wooden roller coaster. Wyoming started regulating rides starting in 1929, and some of the other states followed (though not generally until many years later). In 1973, the federal Consumer Product Safety Commission was created and they began regulating rides as well, although later legislation drastically limited the CPSC's authority. At this point, rides are regulated by a combination of federal, state, and local governments, along with the amusement park industry itself. The federal government only issues regulations for rides that aren't fixed in a permanent location (like those at a county or state fair or other kinds of smaller traveling carnivals), and really they are only able to create guidelines. States can regulate both temporarily placed rides and rides that are fixed in permanent locations, but unsurprisingly, there is a considerable amount of variation between states.

Most states have at least some laws to ensure the safety of amusement park goers. Many of these states license amusement park ride owner-operators and require them to carry liability insurance. Some states also perform equipment inspections (sometimes for a fee), require equipment tests, and set rules about staffing (like age requirements or minimum numbers of staff per ride). This isn't true across the whole country though. While half the states have a regular inspections requirement, ten states leave it up to county governments and/or private inspectors and six states (Alabama, Mississippi, Nevada, Montana, Wyoming, and Utah) don't regulate amusement parks at all.

In general, bigger amusement parks have more independence than smaller ones. In Florida, for example, the state inspects all permanent rides, unless the company that runs the park employs more than a thousand people. This exemption means that parks like Disney World, Busch Gardens, and Universal Studios aren't subject to state inspections and are trusted to self-inspect.

Verruckt, the giant waterslide in Kansas, was built in a state which is known for its light regulatory reach. Before Schlitterbahn opened its Kansas City park, Kansas had no state inspection requirements. In fact, when bills had been proposed, they faced pretty intense opposition from rural lawmakers who were worried that the regulations would negatively impact county fairs and local festivals. In 2008, the Kansas legislature approved a rule that required permanent amusement parks like Schlitterbahn to "self-inspect" its rides annually using a qualified inspector. The state would then have the authority to conduct random audits of the inspection records. The parks were required to keep their records for one year (Hanna 2016).

Caleb Schwab's death on Verruckt prompted the state to strengthen the regulations (KWCH 2017). Under the new rules, amusement park rides would have to be inspected every year by a qualified inspector. In this case, "qualified" means that the inspector would need to either be an engineer with two or more years of amusement park experience, including one year doing inspections or a professional inspector certified by one of the several national boards of amusement park ride safety inspectors. The new regulations also require that parks report injuries to the state.

The law was passed almost unanimously in April of 2017, exactly 8 months after the Schlitterbahn accident. One year after that, in April 2018, the Kansas legislature passed another bill, this time weakening the regulations again. After complaints from rural lawmakers and local officials that the 2017 changes were too broad and were hurting local events, the regulations were amended to set lower requirements for rides at short-term, one-location events run by nonprofit groups and created an exemption for certain types of rides like lower-speed barrel trains and hay-rack rides (AP News 2018).

Schlitterbahn's co-owners Jeffrey Wayne Henry and John Timothy Schooley, the director of operations Tyler Austin Miles, the waterslide's two main designers, and the general contracting company that build Verruckt were indicted on a variety of charges ranging from reckless second-degree murder to involuntary manslaughter to aggravated battery. The Kansas Attorney General alleged that the construction and management of the slide had been handled so poorly and recklessly that those in charge should be held accountable for Caleb's death.

In order to make the case to the grand jury, the Kansas Attorney General showed clips from a Travel Channel show that showed Henry and Schooley bragging about designing the giant waterslide without any technical or engineering qualifications and joking about ignoring safety warnings. Defense attorneys came back and argued that it was inappropriate for the AG to have shown that footage to the grand jury. They claimed that the show was scripted and designed to dramatize the riskiness of the ride so that thrill-seekers would want to visit the park.

The AG also brought in an expert witness, Edward Pribonic, from the American Society of Testing and Materials. The ASTM sets industry standards for rides such as those at Schlitterbahn, and Pribonic testified that Verruckt's design and construction did not meet these industry safety standards. The problem with this is that under the Kansas laws at the time the slide was built, parks were not required to comply with ASTM's standards. The defense was quick to point this out.

Though the indictments made headlines around the country, it is rare that product designers or even operators are held criminally liable for injuries or deaths related to their products. And that was true in this case. The Wyandotte County judge hearing the criminal case ultimately dismissed all the charges, ruling that the AG had used improper methods to sway the grand jury.

Schlitterbahn, the general contracting company, and the ride designers settled a civil case with the Schwab family for almost $20 million.

Discussion Questions

1. To what extent should we be able to trust an industry to self-regulate? What are the pros and cons of doing it like this?
2. What regulations seem reasonable to you for ensuring the safety of amusement rides?
3. Caleb Schwab was the son of a Kansas lawmaker. How do you feel about the fact that it was his death that prompted Kansas to make changes?

Key Terms

- Regulations
- Variation
- Liability
- Audit

For More Information

www.kansascity.com/news/politics-government/article138871638.html
www.esquire.com/news-politics/a23568619/schlitterbahn-freak-accident-caleb-schwab/
www.theatlantic.com/video/index/595981/water-slide/

Notes

1 Of course many federal jobs are in the D.C. metro area, but many aren't. California has the most federal jobs outside of D.C. with almost 150,000 non-postal employees and Vermont has the least with nearly 4,000.
2 Not all states have public employee unions, but even the ones who don't generally have policies that provide for some manner of due process in disciplinary actions.

Works Cited

AP News. (2018, April 27). *Kansas moves to loosen rules for limited-use amusement rides.* https://apnews.com/d7a3fc367c6f41f684e91bea1d5480c3/Kansas-moves-to-loosen-rules-for-limited-use-amusement-rides

City-Data. (n.d.). *Postville, Iowa (IA 52162)* Retrieved October 19, 2020, from http://www.city-data.com/city/Postville-Iowa.html

Dubnick, M. (1995, June 15). Bureaucrat-Bashing Can Lead to Tragedy (Published 1995). *The New York Times.* https://www.nytimes.com/1995/06/15/opinion/l-bureaucrat-bashing-can-lead-to-tragedy-333295.html

Hanna, J. (2016). *Kansas water park operates under limited state regulation.* State Journal Register. https://www.sj-r.com/news/20160813/kansas-water-park-operates-under-limited-state-regulation?template=ampart

KWCH. (2017). *Brownback signs bill to strengthen amusement park regulations.* https://www.kwch.com/content/news/Brownback-signs-bill-to-strengthen-amusement-park-regulations-420290363.html

Layton, L. (2013) Md. exclusion of special ed students affects national scores. *Washington Post.* http://www.washingtonpost.com/local/education/md-exclusion-of-special-ed-students-affects-national-scores/2013/11/24/9b390054-53b2-11e3-9fe0-fd2ca728e67c_story.html.

Lipsky, M. (2010). *Street-level bureaucracy: Dilemmas of the individual in public services.* Russell Sage Foundation. New York.

MacAskill, E. (2011, November 10). *Rick Perry forgets which agency he wants to scrap in Republican debate disaster.* The Guardian. https://www.theguardian.com/world/2011/nov/10/rick-perry-forgets-agency-scrap

Merton, R. K. (1940). Bureaucratic Structure and Personality. *Social Forces, 18*(4), 560–568. https://doi.org/10.2307/2570634

Morris, I. (2014). *War! What is it good for? conflict and the progress of civilization from primates to robots.* Farrar, Straus And Giroux.

Osborne, D., & Gaebler, T. (1994). *Reinventing government : how the entrepreneurial spirit is transforming the public Sector.* Penguin Books, New York.

Reagan, R. (1983). *Evil Empire.* https://voicesofdemocracy.umd.edu/reagan-evil-empire-speech-text/

Reagan, R. (1986). *President's News Conference.* https://www.reaganfoundation.org/ronald-reagan/reagan-quotes-speeches/news-conference-1/

Tausanovich, C., & Warshaw, C. (2014). Representation in Municipal Government. *The American Political Science Review, 108*(3), 605–641.

US Bureau of Labor Statistics. (2020a). *Union Members Summary.* https://www.bls.gov/news.release/union2.nr0.htm

US Bureau of Labor Statistics. (2020b). *Employee Benefits in the United States.* https://www.bls.gov/news.release/pdf/ebs2.pdf

Von Mises, L. (2007). *Bureaucracy.* Indianapolis, Ind. Liberty Fund. (Original work published 1944)

Wais, E. (2005). *Trained Incapacity: Thorstein Veblen and Kenneth Burke | KB Journal.* Kbjournal. Org. https://kbjournal.org/wais

11

LOCAL GOVERNMENTS

Alexander De Tocqueville viewed local governments in the U.S. as sort of mini-republics. He saw them as civic entities in which citizens were closest to government and in which government reflected accurately what citizens desired. In some ways he was right. Local governments wield actual power and are responsible for important programs and services. Yet, local governments are far from idea. They tend to have low voter turnout for their elections. Most localities are constrained by Dillon's Rule. Local governments today in fact face significant challenges, most notably dealing with budget shortfalls.

Now, imagine you are running a small town with a small budget and you get a phone call that thousands of people are about to descend on your five hotel rooms. What decisions do you need to make? What resources do you have? These are real questions that had to be addressed in New Mexico recently, and we get into all the details in the first section. We then move across the country to Florida where we use Clearwater as an example case of a town deciding what kind of local leadership system that they want. Finally, we trek up to Iowa to another small town, one that was almost devastated a while back by an immigration raid. We finish the chapter by discussing the impact a large raid has on small towns and how this particular town recovered eventually.

Handling an "Alien" Invasion in a Small Desert Town

In June 2019, a video game streamer and college student named Matty Roberts listened to an episode of the podcast The Joe Rogan Experience that featured a conspiracy theorist that claimed to have worked on projects involving alien spacecraft at a secret underground facility located at Area 51. Inspired, he created a meme and Facebook event encouraging people to storm the facility to "see them aliens" because "they can't stop us all." Roberts made it clear that it was a joke, however the meme and the related event went viral reaching far across various social media platforms. Almost two million people RSVP'd to the event. It became such a thing that a remix of the #1 song of the summer, Old Town Road was made all about the raid and beer company Bud Light promised free beer to any alien that made it out of the facility.

Area 51 is the name of the highly classified U.S. government facility located in Nevada and is part of the Nevada Test and Training Range, which is part of the Nellis Air Force Base Complex. According to the Air Force, which operates the facility, it is a training site that allows the military to develop and try out new aircraft and weapons systems. It makes sense why the site is so secretive, right? We don't want our adversaries to get the heads up about the new military technology that we are developing. But human nature being what it is, when things are secret, some people are going to come up with elaborate stories about what is being hidden from the public. Many of these stories have become conspiracy theories centered on extraterrestrials, or aliens. There are rumors that Area 51 houses a crashed alien spaceship and its passengers that were recovered from Roswell and that the site is used to meet and/or develop projects with aliens to develop new technology.

While Matty Roberts was clear from the beginning that the event was intended as a joke, some of the people who responded didn't seem to have gotten the message. The United States Air Force issued a warning to those who may actually be tempted to show up, "Area 51 is an open training range for the U.S. Air Force, and we would discourage anyone from trying to come into the area where we train American armed forces" (Puzzo 2019). Attempting to enter the base without authorization can come with steep fines or jail time. Trying to force your way in could be met with force to keep you out. The United States military doesn't mess around when it comes to security.

While the Air Force is well equipped to handle a bunch of Naruto-running[1] alien-liberators who took an internet joke too seriously, there was more at stake for the local population. The Nellis Air Force Base Complex (which is roughly the size of Connecticut), is in a remote part of Nevada, but there are a handful of small towns surrounding it. The closest town is a tiny little outpost called Rachel. Home to just 54 people, Rachel, Nevada enjoys an outsized amount of attention as a tourist spot due to its location by Area 51 and positioning on the "Extraterrestrial Highway" (Highway 375). There is a tourist shop, an alien-themed restaurant and bar, and a small hotel with 12 rooms. There is no school or post office, no gas station or grocery store (Wikipedia 2019).

The people who live in Rachel were split on how to feel about the potential onslaught of tourists. Some, including the owners of the restaurant/bar and hotel welcomed the business. After all, it was an opportunity for them to make more money than they usually do. Hoping to help accommodate the visitors, in addition to the 12 hotel rooms, they cleared the way for RV and tent camping spots and ordered port-a-potties so at least people would have somewhere to go to the bathroom and a water truck so hydration was available. When Matty Roberts suggested they turn the event into a music festival, some of Rachel's citizens got even more excited at the potential. Near(ish)by town, Hiko, Nevada also started planning events for the same weekend, expecting spillover from the visitors that Rachel wouldn't be able to handle. Hiko, Nevada is home to 119 people and has so little economic activity that it is listed on several ghost town registers.

Other residents were not so enthusiastic about the possibility of people (dozens? hundreds? thousands? aliens?) showing up on their doorsteps. They had concerns about what kind of damage a large crowd, with nowhere to stay, few restrooms available, no grocery or convenience stores, one bar/restaurant and one water truck could do to their quiet little area. Would people try to sleep or mingle on their property? What about their fields and animals? Lincoln County, which houses Rachel as well as Hiko, is home to more cows than people and ranching is the primary source of income for many of the area's residents. If fences got broken and cattle got out … well, that could be catastrophic for a small ranch. Further, things like the electrical grid, the cell phone towers, and the internet lines aren't built to handle that many people. What if they all went down?

In preparation, the Lincoln County commissioners drafted an emergency declaration that could be used to request assistance from the state if they had needed it. This, if accepted by the Governor, could have triggered resources like additional law enforcement being sent to the area and supplies and equipment to help local response agencies. The emergency declaration basically works as an official bat-signal to the state that something is happening that is too big for the local government to handle and that they need help. They are often used for weather emergencies, like in the aftermath of blizzards or hurricanes. They are not often used to corral alien hunters.

The ability to appeal to "higher" levels of government for help when there is a situation is one of the benefits of federalism. Whether it is a hurricane, a financial crisis, or yes, even the potential influx of internet junkies hoping to prove the existence of aliens, states tend to have more resources than localities. And the federal government has more resources than states. While many topics are best handled locally, it isn't always possible. So, even though the giant flood of alien hunters didn't end up appearing in Nevada, the preparations and procedures remain no less relevant—and appreciated by at least 54 people.

Discussion Questions

1. If people had shown up for the event and end up damaging the town, should any responsibility have been placed with Matty Roberts?

2. Does the Air Force have a duty to help out a town that is located so close to their base?
3. If part of the town's population wants to hold a big event but part of it doesn't, how do you balance those desires to make everyone happy?
4. What other types of situations might require a locality to declare an emergency before anything even happens?

Key Terms

- Area 51
- Emergency declaration
- Federalism

For More Information

www.vox.com/culture/2019/9/27/20879010/storm-area-51-alienstock-event-photos
www.bbc.com/news/world-us-canada-49667295

Council-Manager or Strong Mayor? Clearwater, FL Decides

Just like the majority of the cities and towns in Florida, Clearwater operates using a council-manager form of government. In a council-manager system, council members are the leaders, duly elected to represent the community and develop policy that is responsive to the needs of the community. The council, as a centralized legislative body, does things like approve the budget, determine the local tax rate, and strategize on the community's long-term goals and major projects. In this form of government, the city council hires a professional city manager to oversee the delivery of public services. The city manager's job is to serve the council and the community by administering the projects and programs that are developed and funded by the city council.

This is a popular form of governance, making up almost 60% of municipal governments (Ballotpedia n.d.). The number of governments using a council-manager system has increased over the past couple of decades as part of an overall trend toward professionalization in municipal administration and as state and federal laws and regulations requiring transparency and accountability increased. There are several other cities in Florida though, such as Tampa and St. Petersburg that use a mayor-council system. In the mayor-council system, remember, the mayor is elected separately from the city council and (at least in the strong-mayor form) has administrative authority over the executive branch. They can hire and fire department heads, control spending, coordinate projects ... and, often, negotiate deals on behalf of their city.

It was this last feature that piqued the interest of some members of the Clearwater business and real estate community in 2018. They argued that Clearwater should change over to a strong mayor system so that they would have an elected mayor who, unencumbered by Florida's open meetings law, would be able to talk to developers and potential business interests and potentially put Clearwater on the path toward being more of a player in the region and across the state. Any change in the system of governance would have to be put to a vote of the people in Clearwater, though. So, this group of business leaders, along with the Clearwater Downtown Partnership, put together a political action committee (PAC) called the Accountable Government PAC. They were able to get the issue put on the ballot in 2018 and raised over $163,000 to support it, which is a pretty hefty amount for a local ballot initiative (Clifford 2018).

But not everyone was so sure that this change would be a good idea. Opponents were afraid that putting the general administrative power in the hands of a politician (who might be influenced by things like campaign contributions) would be a dangerous move. A rival PAC was convened, and the No Boss Mayor PAC raised over $90,000 to fight the change.

Both sides of the issue made some good points. After all, there are pros and cons to each of the options in Clearwater. Council-manager systems are less susceptible to political influence and provide a level of stability and expertise that the other systems often lack. But it is more difficult to hold officials accountable and it is sometimes confusing for citizens who are looking to ask questions or provide feedback on policies or problems. On the other hand, a strong mayor system has a more clearly visible leader. This helps the public know who the person is that they are supposed to talk to and to hold that person accountable for the decisions that they make. It is also true that elected mayors are able to made decisions and affect change more quickly than city managers.

The Accountable Government PAC came out in full force, buying up television spots and sending out mailers that argued that the future of Clearwater depended on this change. A week before the election they took the rhetoric a step further, warning voters (misleadingly) that voting no on the referendum would result in unelected bureaucrats with no term limits making all the decisions for the city. The No Boss Mayor PAC took a different approach, running a grassroots campaign that didn't include television advertising but relied instead on a team of volunteers to knock on doors and talk to voters directly and to hold up signs in high traffic areas.

The residents of Clearwater pretty clearly decided that one side had the better argument. When they voted in November of 2018, 59% of the 42,053 voters rejected the change, opting to keep the council-manager system under which they had been operating for almost 100 years (McManus 2018).

Did the voters in Clearwater make the correct choice? Or did they mess up and miss out on the opportunity to become more of a powerhouse in their region? A paper published in a 2014 issue of the American Political Science Review (Tausanovitch and Warshaw 2014) suggests that, at least in some ways, it may not have mattered. Researchers Chris Tausanovitch of UCLA and Christopher Warshaw of MIT conducted a study of 1,600 cities and towns around the U.S. They used surveys that asked the residents of those towns about their political leanings and policy preferences and then compared those results to information about the policies actually enacted by each individual local government entity. It turned out that ALL of the municipal governments were pretty good at passing policies that aligned with the preferences of their constituents. This was equally true for council-manager systems and for mayor-council ones.

The APSR study found that responsiveness doesn't vary systematically between the systems, but didn't look at the relative efficiency differences. After all, one of the biggest arguments put forth by the Accountable Government PAC was that a strong mayor would be able to more efficiently and effectively grow Clearwater into a regional force. An earlier study in the Southern Economic Journal looked at this question more specifically. They looked at cities like they were businesses and the services they provide (police, fire, refuse) as products. They also took into account the salaries for the city manager and mayor in the council-manager systems and the mayor in mayor-council systems. Comparing the costs and services for each city led the researchers to conclude that neither form of government is always, or even almost always, the more efficient one. They also found that mayors in the council-manager systems are actually far stronger than they are given credit for.

For Clearwater, the goal now is to look forward. The Accountable Government PAC acknowledged that while they were disappointed in the results and stood by their claims that a strong mayor would have been good for Clearwater, the voters had spoken. In an interview with the Tampa Bay Times, Mayor George Cretekos said, "I hope all residents and others in the city will work together now within this preferred framework so we can continue to offer stable non-partisan and professional management."

Discussion Questions

1. Do you know what kind of system they have in your town/city? If not, find out!
2. Is it anti-democratic to have a professional city manager doing things and making decisions rather than an elected Mayor?
3. Does it surprise you that research shows that municipal governments tend to be pretty good at their jobs? Why or why not?

Key Terms

- Council-manager system
- City manager
- Strong mayor
- Mayor-council system
- Political Action Committee

For More Information:

https://icma.org/documents/council-manager-form-government-what-how-it-works-and-benefits-your-community-brochure
www.cambridge.org/core/services/aop-cambridge-core/content/view/924BD
D2C2ECD0CC9B42E5A19776BC9C3/S0003055414000318a.pdf/representation_
in_municipal_government.pdf
www.jstor.org/stable/1060487?seq=10#metadata_info_tab_contents

Postville, IA: A Town Recovers from a Major Immigration Raid

On August 7, 2019, immigration enforcement authorities raided seven food processing plants across six cities in Mississippi, detaining 680 workers in the biggest single-day single-state sweep in U.S. history. At one of the plants, the arrests meant the loss of nearly half of the workers on the floor, causing a shutdown of operations for the day.

The operation in Mississippi targeted food processing plants, which have long relied on immigrant labor to do the demanding and often unpleasant work of cleaning, deboning, and cutting animals apart into the pieces that we see at the grocery store or that get used by restaurants and other edible food sources. The Mississippi raids, however, were hardly the first that the U.S. has seen. And because the majority of these kinds of food processing facilities are located in small towns, the sudden loss of dozens, or even hundreds, of people can have a devastating effect on the operations and economy of these towns.

On May 12, 2008, residents of tiny Postville, Iowa (population just over 2,000) were surprised to hear the sound of helicopters overhead. People looked out doors and windows, wondering if maybe the National Guard was doing a demonstration or something. It wasn't the Guard though. The immigration enforcement authorities were descending on the local kosher meatpacking plant, in a huge operation to pick up undocumented workers. Nearly 400 of the plant's workers were arrested (Crowder and Elmer 2018).

We can argue all day about how immigration enforcement should be handled in the U.S., but that isn't really a local government issue. What is though, is what a town does when 20% of its population disappears one day. After the raid in Postville, when these hundreds of undocumented workers were arrested, suddenly a fifth of the town's people were not there to do things like pay rent, or eat at the restaurant, or buy things at the stores. The enrollment at the local school dropped precipitously. And, as this happened in 2008, the whole thing went down as the nation was already suffering from effects of the Great Recession.

Rural areas, such as Northern Iowa where Postville is located, have seen a pretty significant population decrease over the past few decades. Metropolitan areas, cities with at least 50,000 people and the counties that surround them and that are economically linked to them make up around 35% of all counties, but since 2008 they have eaten up over 98% of job and population growth (Mitchell 2018). Between 2008 and 2017, more than half of rural counties either stagnated or shrank, population-wise (Swenson 2019). For towns such as Postville, this means that having a large, steady employer like Agri-Processors, the kosher meat processing plant involved in the raid, is vital for the community's existence. Remember that not only do these kinds of plants employ a significant chunk of the town's residents, other businesses in town like the grocery store, restaurant, gas station, hardware store, and the like rely on the paychecks that the plant workers receive to fuel their own businesses. It is all connected.

The goal of these immigration sweeps is to arrest and potentially deport people who are here working when they don't have the proper authorization, but it is also to deter people from doing the same in the future. This tactic may work, but that is for another textbook to deal with. The question for those of us looking at local government has more to do with the impact that these policies have on the communities involved. Prior to Agri-Processors opening in 1987, Postville had been like so many dying Midwestern towns. When the new business swept in, taking over a defunct meatpacking plant, it had brought with it jobs as well as a multicultural group of new residents such that rural Midwestern towns rarely see. Agri-Processors was a kosher processing company, and a significant population of Hasidic Jews followed it there. At the peak, there were 100 Hasidic families living in Postville. Further, a steady stream of Eastern European and then Latin American workers poured in to fill the jobs. New businesses sprung up to support these new people, a kosher deli, a Guatemalan restaurant, a Mexican Vaquero. Postville was suddenly one of the most diverse towns in Iowa.

When so many of Agri-Processors' employees, a full third of its workforce, were taken away and its management under fire for hiring undocumented workers, it was unsurprisingly unable to continue operating and filed for bankruptcy. In addition to the workers swept up in the raid, others who were unable to find work in the small town left. Houses and businesses were left vacant and there were no potential buyers. Property values fell drastically and the local government couldn't bring in enough tax revenue to pay the bills. Remember that local governments are highly dependent on property taxes to survive. Postville was on the edge of a complete collapse.

It didn't collapse though. And, interestingly enough, Postville was saved by the same thing that got it going in the first place—immigrants. In 2009, a Jewish Canadian company purchased and reopened the plant under a new name, Agri Star. The new management recruited immigrants from all over the world to come to Postville to work. This time, though, they were more careful about operating inside of the strict immigration laws. They also recruited groups of Somalis, who were living as refugees in Minnesota, to come work. Refugees can work in the U.S. legally.

Postville now is even more diverse than it was before the raid. In 2017, almost half of its population is Latino, Hispanic, Black, Asian, or Native American (City-Data n.d.). Many of the residents are recent immigrants and refugees from Somalia and Latin America. This may not seem super diverse compared to some other parts of the country or many large cities, but for Iowa, which is almost entirely non-Hispanic white, Postville is an anomaly. And if it wasn't for this diversity, Postville would have died in 2008 along with Agri-Processors. Agri-Processors did try to stay afloat after the raid. They tried to attract new groups of workers, ones with the proper paperwork to work legally in the U.S., but they simply ran out of time and money. The jobs available didn't attract American workers. When Agri Star came in, they realized this set about bringing back foreign workers; the difference is that this time it was done legally.

In the current political climate, it seems that we have not seen the end of these large-scale immigration raids. The troubles that Postville went through, trying to stay alive as a community after so many of its residents simply disappeared one day should serve as a learning opportunity for other small towns that rely so heavily on one large company that may employ undocumented workers.

Discussion Questions

1. Should employers who hire undocumented immigrants bear more responsibility when these kinds of raids happen?
2. What are the reasons that we might expect raids such as the one in Postville to increase moving forward?
3. How can industries in small towns attract workers that aren't at risk for getting in this kind of trouble?
4. Should the law enforcement take the potential impact of a large-scale raid on a community into consideration before doing massive immigration sweeps?

Key Terms

- Immigration
- Undocumented workers

- Great recession
- Sociodemographics

For More Information:

https://carsey.unh.edu/publication/rural-depopulation

Note

1 The Naruto Run, based on the Japanese anime series Naruto, was part of the original joke. It is a style of running that involves tipping your torso forward and extending your arms behind you and running really fast. The idea is that it gives you more speed. It does not.

Works Cited

Ballotpedia. (n.d.). *Council-manager government.* Retrieved October 19, 2020, from https://ballotpedia.org/Council-manager_government

Chao, G., & Gardner, P. (n.d.). *How Central is Work to Young Adults?* Retrieved October 19, 2020, from https://ceri.msu.edu/_assets/pdfs/young-pro-pdfs/work_young_adults.pdf

Clifford, D. (2018). *Strong mayor in Clearwater or not? Backers, opponents take their cases to residents.* Tampa Bay Times. https://www.tampabay.com/news/pinellas/clearwater/strong-mayor-in-clearwater-or-not-backers-opponents-take-their-cases-to-residents-20181002/

Crowder, C., & Elmer, M. (2018). *A decade after a massive raid nabbed 400 undocumented workers, this tiny town fights to reclaim its identity.* Des Moines Register. https://www.desmoinesregister.com/story/news/investigations/2018/05/10/postville-immigration-raid-10-year-anniversary-town-reclaims-identity/587995002/

McManus, T. (2018). *Clearwater voters resoundingly reject strong mayor government.* Tampa Bay Times. https://www.tampabay.com/blogs/baybuzz/2018/11/05/clearwater-strong-mayor/

Mitchell, T. (2018, May 22). *Demographic and economic trends in urban, suburban and rural communities.* Pew Research Center. https://www.pewsocialtrends.org/2018/05/22/demographic-and-economic-trends-in-urban-suburban-and-rural-communities/

Puzzo, A. (2019, July 17). *'Storming' Area 51: Internet meme or an actual threat?* Air Force Times. https://www.airforcetimes.com/news/your-air-force/2019/07/17/storming-area-51-internet-meme-or-an-actual-threat/

Swenson, D. (2019). *Most of America's rural areas are doomed to decline.* The Conversation. https://theconversation.com/most-of-americas-rural-areas-are-doomed-to-decline-115343

Wikipedia. (2019, October 22). *Rachel.* https://en.wikipedia.org/wiki/Rachel

12

REGIONAL GOVERNANCE

The central issues of regional politics boils down to the gap that exists between local and state governments. Local governments were founded and organized during a horse and buggy era, and those organizational structures do not also make for a rational fit with modern realities. This gap becomes particularly noticeable in areas with a lot of people spread out over a wide space.

When you think about a lot of people spread out, you might immediately think of somewhere like Los Angeles. And to be fair, there are a lot of people there and it does spread out over dozens and dozens of miles. But does LA actually have sprawl? Maybe not. That's what we start out with in this chapter. To the east, another large metropolitan area, Houston, does have quite a bit of sprawl and an increasing amount of non-permeable surface area. The middle section of this chapter talks about some of the potential implications of this, including increased flooding. We end by talking about Tiebout's theory and how it works (or doesn't) in terms of public schools and community satisfaction.

The Sprawliest Sprawl—Not Los Angeles?

Urban sprawl. It is one of the most pressing issues for policymakers in urban areas. And no American city exemplifies sprawl like Los Angeles. Right? Just ask the two million results that come back on "Los Angeles sprawl" on Google. Heck, there is a good chance that your state and local politics textbook uses LA as their prime example.

It makes sense. Los Angeles is huge—the metro area is a gigantic 4,850 square miles, and if you look at the larger, "touching" area (basically from the border of San Diego County up to Santa Barbara), we are talking about almost

34,000 square miles. To put that in perspective, it is about the same size as South Carolina and bigger than all of the New England states except for Maine.

LA is also known for ridiculous traffic and inordinate amounts of pollution. In 2018, Los Angeles drivers spent an average of 128 hours stuck in traffic, and the 101 and 405 freeways count among the most congested in the world (Chiland 2019). And the traffic isn't just annoying and inconvenient, according to the American Lung Association, the Los Angeles metro area has the worst ozone pollution and almost the worst particle pollution in the whole country (American Lung Association 2018). No wonder people equate it with sprawl.

According to New York University's Thomas Liadley, though, LA is "the least sprawling metro in the country" (Romero 2015). How on earth can this be possible? Well, according to Laidley and his fellow researcher Richard Florida, it largely comes down to how you define sprawl. Laidley's main point is that Los Angeles is just flat out too crowded to count as sprawly. In fact, with over 7,000 people per square mile, Los Angeles is the most densely populated metro areas in the U.S. This is different than it being the most densely populated city—sprawl necessarily includes outlying suburbs and exurbs that are often not within city limits. L.A. has lots of suburbs and basically no empty space between them.

Compare this with other areas of the country. For example, I was recently in Sanford, North Carolina visiting my in-laws. Sanford is in Lee County which is part of the greater "triangle" area of Raleigh-Durham. It is also about the same distance to Charlotte and Fayetteville. To get to my mother-in-law's house, we flew into the Raleigh-Durham airport. We then had to drive for about an hour, starting through the relatively congested area around the airport, then spending a while driving through far more sparsely populated areas before getting to Sanford itself. Then, the neighborhood where she actually lives is another fifteen minutes from central Sanford, outside of city limits and as geographically and socioeconomically removed as possible while still calling itself Sanford. Again, this drive goes through very sparsely populated areas. The neighborhood, while large (2,500 acres, containing more than one thousand homes), does not have any business or industry to sustain it economically. Sanford, while bigger (a little over 8,500 households) and containing several businesses and industrial sites has become more and more linked to the larger cities that surround it. Housing is cheaper, one can get more of a small-town feel, and crime is lower, but it is still reasonable for many to commute to Raleigh or Charlotte or Fayetteville for work.

Many of the most sprawling areas in the U.S. are located in the Southeast. In fact, all of the top (bottom?) sprawliest metro areas are in warm areas (Goodyear 2014).

1. Hickory/Lenoir/Morganton, North Carolina
2. Atlanta/Sandy Springs/Marietta, Georgia
3. Clarksville, Tennessee/Kentucky
4. Prescott, Arizona

5. Nashville-Davidson/Murfreesboro/Franklin, Tennessee
6. Baton Rouge, Louisiana
7. Riverside-San Bernardino/Ontario, California
8. Greenville/Mauldin-Easley, South Carolina
9. Augusta/Richmond County, Georgia
10. Kingsport/Bristol/Bristol, Tennessee/Virginia

A U.S. Geological Survey study in 2014 found that population growth in the Southeast U.S. has been as much as 40 percent faster than the rest of the country (Stolark 2014). 77 million people have joined this region in the past 60 years. There are a few reasons for this. First, there is a distinct lack of geographical limitation to sprawl in many of these areas. You aren't running into oceans or mountain ranges on all sides. Second, many of these metro areas are not so culturally focused on ecologically friendly development. The local and state governments in the South are more concerned with growth and economic development. Finally, the U.S. has simply seen a demographic trend where people are moving to the warmer areas of the country.

Certainly, Los Angeles has gained population over the years. Heck, from 1920 until 1930, Los Angeles County went from just over 900,000 residents to over 2.2 million. That's a ridiculous gain of 1.3 million people in only ten years. And then by 1970, there were over seven million people living in Los Angeles County and just about ten million living there today. These are huge population gains, but notice that we are talking here about Los Angeles County, not the metro area. The county has lines. So, when the population grew and added six million people in 50 years, all of those people were inside of the county lines, so the area necessarily got denser. That isn't to say that the population didn't spill over those lines and grow outward. It did. The LA metro area had almost sixteen million residents as of the 2010 census (United States Census Bureau 2010).

Just because Los Angeles has the population density distributed regularly enough to keep it off of Liadley's list doesn't mean that it doesn't suffer from many of the same problems that it would if it was considered to have more sprawl. Indeed, it has all of the traffic and air pollution problems associated with the drawbacks of sprawl. It also doesn't have some of the perks of a more compact city, like effective public transportation. What we can learn from L.A. is that increasing density is not the end-all-be-all solution to sprawl that some textbooks might have you believe. A city can be dense, but still have many of the problems typically associated with sprawl.

Discussion Questions

1. How much sprawl is there in your area? Is it sprawl in the traditional sense or in Liadley's conception of sprawl?

2. If making a city more dense isn't necessarily the answer for decreasing traffic and pollution, what can we do?
3. Are some cities just too big? How can we encourage people to live in other places?

Key Terms

- Sprawl
- Metropolitan area
- Population density
- Population growth
- Suburbs
- Exurbs

For More Information

http://uar.sagepub.com/content/early/2015/02/07/1078087414568812. abstract?rss=1

www.wired.com/2015/06/los-angeles-building-ages-map/

www.accessmagazine.org/fall-2010/density-doesnt-tell-us-sprawl/

The Houston Metro Area: Flood City U.S.A.

In 2017, Hurricane Harvey set US rainfall records, stalling out over southern Texas and pouring more than five feet of rain over the area. It used to be that most of the deaths we would see from hurricanes were caused by storm surge (the sudden rush of ocean water onto land caused by the pressure of the storm—picture a hair dryer aimed at a bowl of water, pushing it over edges), but 65 of the 68 people killed by Harvey were killed by freshwater flooding (Crow 2018). More than half of these fatalities were in the Houston metropolitan area.

Tragic, unforeseeable act of nature? Well, more and more experts have been arguing that we are making flooding worse through urban sprawl. According to the National Weather Service, damage from freshwater flooding has totaled almost $8 billion per year for the past 30 years, and two thirds of claims made on flood insurance are the result of freshwater flooding (National Weather Service 2014). Some of this damage comes from rivers and creeks rising up over their banks, but experts are seeing that much of the damage is not coming from waterways, but is the result of man-made development. Streets, parking lots, driveways, roofs, and other impermeable surfaces have taken over landscapes like fields and wetlands that used to absorb rainfall and drainage, giving the water little choice but to rush around neighborhoods and into homes.

Houston has found itself in a particularly tight spot. Due to its location and climate, major storms hitting the area are relatively common. Part of that, of course, is the cost of living on the Gulf Coast. In addition, people keep moving there. Lots of people. According to the Census bureau, from 2017 to 2018, 251 people moved to Houston EVERY SINGLE DAY (Egan 2019). That is over 90,000 people in just one year. Cities like growth. More people mean more jobs and demand for products and services and economic growth. But people need places to live, and Houston, with its aversion to regulating development, has seen a substantial amount of sprawl. As a result, Houston, has seen a substantial reduction in wetlands and prairies over the past several years. In fact, between 1992 and 2010, urban development caused a 29% loss of wetland area (Campoy and Yanofsky 2017). Many areas that were once covered by deep-rooted prairie grass, which has the ability to absorb huge amounts of water, have disappeared in favor of human development. For example, northwest of Houston, an area called the Katy Prairie used to boast around 600,000 acres of undeveloped land that took on rain water has recently been reduced to about 150,000 acres after housing and commercial developments were approved for the property. A report by the National Academies of Sciences, Engineering, and Medicine pointed out (not long before Hurricane Harvey), that the combination of low-lying land, clay-based soil, and urban sprawl is a particularly bad one, putting Houston at extreme risk for catastrophic flooding (ScienceDaily 2018).

Though Houston provides us with a stark example, they are far from alone. From Madison, Wisconsin, to New York City to Omaha, Nebraska, scientists are warning that urban flooding is only going to get worse. Not everyone agrees with this assessment though. In fact, the head of the flood control district that covers Houston dismisses the report completely, and many of his colleagues agree with him. They argue that the standards for allowing new development on prairie and wetlands are likely fine and that the recent uptick in storms are simply a freak occurrence and that, if anything, we should simply be looking to upgrade infrastructure like levees and flood walls.

After a major flood event in 2001, Houston officials did try to tighten up some regulations about building on the most vulnerable parts of the floodplains, those closest to the bayous, and they were promptly sued by groups of developers and residents. It is a tricky situation—the city's leadership doesn't want to discourage development. They are well aware that businesses who find their rules too strict may simply leave Houston in favor of a city with fewer restrictions. This is one of the enduring struggles of government—you might want to make changes that may help mitigate potential future problems, but if those changes have immediate negative results, such as with the loss of business and development, it is politically more difficult to justify making those changes. It might be outright political suicide for elected or appointed officials.

It is true that flooding is hardly a new problem for Houston. One can look back to the 1930s for evidence that residents and the local government were seeking relief from flooding caused by rainwater. The difference now is that millions more people live there, with billions of dollars in property they want to protect. On top of that the Gulf of Mexico is getting warmer, which means it is likely that Houston and other Gulf areas will see more storms and storms that are wetter, dropping more and more rainwater on them. Other cities, such as Broward County, FL and Milwaukee, WI are starting to prepare for an increase flood events, and many Houston residents are hoping to see the same. Until then, the reports indicate, there is a very good chance that the Houston area will flood more and more often.

Discussion Questions

1. What responsibility should local governments have for using climate change as a factor in their planning schemas?
2. How should government entities balance the needs of growth, business, and economic development with the need for sustainability?
3. When people disagree about the urgency of planning for climate change, who should have the ultimate authority?
4. To what extent should elected officials listen to scientists versus listening to their citizens when they don't agree?

Key Terms

- Storm surge
- Urban sprawl
- Impermeable surfaces
- Floodplains
- Development

For More Information

https://cdr.umd.edu/urban-flooding-report
https://www.ncbi.nlm.nih.gov/pmc/articles/PMC5288645/
https://www.nature.com/articles/s41586-018-0676-z

Tiebout Gets Schooled: The Indirect Benefits of Public Schools on Community Satisfaction

In 1956, Charles Tiebout, an economist, wrote "A Pure Theory of Local Expenditures" (Tiebout 1956). In it, he posits that people have a sort of market relationship with local governments where we are the consumers and they are the providers. He said that each locality offers different goods (services mostly) at different prices (tax rates) and that as consumers we can "shop" around for the goods and prices that we want simply by moving. Our ability and willingness to do this creates competition and forces local governments to create optimal environments to attract residents.

In order for his model to work, Tiebout hypothesizes seven assumptions. They are:

- People are fully mobile and can/will move to a community where their preferences are best met
- People have full knowledge of the policies that create differences between communities
- There are plenty of communities for people to choose from
- There are no barriers based on employment opportunities
- The services provided in communities (and also any bad characteristics) stay fully within that community and never spill over the border
- There is an idea community size
- Communities will act to reach their ideal size

One way to look at this is to imagine two households, one with children and one without. Presume that the family with children values public schools and is willing to pay a premium for this service, but that the family without children would prefer their tax dollars be spent on something else since they aren't using the public schools anyway. In Tiebout's conception, the first family would move to a town where there is a school and the second would move to a town without a school. Eventually, town A would be made up of families with children and town B would consist of families without children and everyone will have gotten what they want. This is, of course, an overly-simplified way of illustrating the model. People have multiple preferences to add in to the calculus, and towns spend money on many different services. This example should give you the basic idea of where Tiebout was going though.

The assumptions that he makes have received considerable criticism over the years. It isn't always so easy to move and there are often high costs associated with moving—think about hiring a moving company or even a U-Haul, paying a deposit and first month's rent on an apartment (or a down payment and closing costs on a house), and the time it takes to pack up and move a household to a different location. And what if you have family in your current location that you don't want to move away from? Further, are you going to be able to get a job in your new location? If you are a ski instructor, you might have a hard time moving to Alabama, or if your experience is in flood control and management, it may be harder to find work in a desert environment.

And really, do people truly have perfect information about the options and services provided in all of the available communities? People do make choices about where to live that are in part based on the availability of services in an area, but PERFECT information is unlikely to be realistic in any real-world situation. Public policy is an intricate beast, and communities are complex systems made up of multiple policies, some of which even the most engaged of citizens aren't well versed on.

Research also indicates that sometimes benefits are more complicated than they may first seem. Let's go back to the public school example. The childless family didn't want to live in the community that was using tax money to pay for schools that they wouldn't be using. Makes sense, right? And many communities do offer tax breaks for specific demographic groups, like senior citizens, to lighten their burden in consideration of their not benefitting from public schools. And how can you argue with that? Maybe people shouldn't have to pay for a resource that they don't use.

The other side of this is that it is generally good for everyone in a community if the population is educated, and while no one really disputes that, this is true it doesn't really do much to convince people that they should pay for a service that they don't need. A 2012 study in the Journal of Urban Affairs found that there may actually be more benefits than just these general ones (Neal and Watling Neal 2012).

Authors Zachary Neal and Jennifer Watling Neal looked at survey responses from 20,000 people from 26 different cities around the U.S. The survey had asked the respondents about the things in their communities that make them happy living there. What they discovered is that there is a strong connection between community satisfaction and school quality and that this held true even for people who don't have kids. As the authors conclude, "public school quality uniquely contributes to community satisfaction," even above and beyond other variables like home ownership, job availability, and other community characteristics.

Their take on these results is that public schools serve a greater function in a community than simply as educational institutions. As community institutions school provide tangible benefits like space for night classes, gyms for fitness classes, and libraries for ESL resources. And then there are less tangible things too. A good public school system creates a network of involved parents and communities with networks of engaged members is one that is generally a nicer place to live.

The effect that Neal and Watling Neal found only holds for the neighborhood public schools and not for charter or private schools. Of course, these other types of schools can offer all of the same tangible benefits as public schools can but the authors point out that there is one big difference that gives public schools the edge when it comes to the intangible things. Private schools and charter schools often draw from a far broader population, not necessarily bounded by the neighborhood where they are located. The authors argue that public schools' relationship with a geographical location is such that members of the community become bound together in a multitude of ways that are also related to the geographic location. Essentially, families get involved in their kids' schools and then they get involved in other things like the neighborhood association and the public library. Then, their neighbors, even the ones without kids, who run into these families at the neighborhood association meeting or the library become more familiar with what the schools are doing and they become better community members themselves.

Tiebout didn't account for indirect benefits like this. This isn't to say that there is no indication that Tiebout's model doesn't work sometimes. There have been studies in suburban Michigan, for example, where you do see people "voting with their feet" and moving between communities to find one that maximizes the things that they value. Another study, by Sandra Black, found that housing prices vary across school districts and that parents are willing to shell out almost 3% more money for a house in order to be in a district with 5% higher average test scores (Black 1999). So, some level of sorting is happening, just as Tiebout had predicted. And maybe, if we were to look more closely at indirect benefits, we would see even more of this.

Discussion Questions

1. What do you think of Tiebout's assumptions? Are they a reasonable approximation of how people make decisions?
2. What kinds of services could a government offer that would make you want to move to one town over another?
3. Public schools confer indirect positive benefits on communities. Are there other public entities that might act similarly?

Key Terms

- Tiebout hypothesis
- Competition
- Mobility
- School Districts
- Community satisfaction

For More Information:

www.tandfonline.com/doi/abs/10.1111/j.1467-9906.2011.00595.x
https://academic.oup.com/qje/article-abstract/114/2/577/1844232

Works Cited

American Lung Association (2018). *Most Polluted Cities, Then and Now.* https://www.lung.org/blog/sota-then-and-now

Black, S. E. (1999). Do Better Schools Matter? Parental Valuation of Elementary Education. *The Quarterly Journal of Economics, 114*(2), 577–599. https://doi.org/10.1162/003355399556070

Campoy, A., & Yanofsky, D. (2017). *Houston's flooding shows what happens when you ignore science and let developers run rampant.* Quartz. https://qz.com/1064364/hurricane-harvey-houstons-flooding-made-worse-by-unchecked-urban-development-and-wetland-destruction/

Chiland, E. (2019, February 13). *LA drivers face nation's fifth-worst traffic, says report.* Curbed LA; Curbed LA. https://la.curbed.com/2019/2/13/18222225/los-angeles-traffic-worst-nation-hours

Crow, K. (2018). *What date did Hurricane Harvey make landfall? Here are key facts from the Coastal Bend.* Caller-Times. https://www.caller.com/story/news/local/2018/05/21/what-know-hurricane-harvey-and-its-effect-coastal-bend-rockport-port-aransas-corpus-christi/581670002/

Egan, J. (2019). *Houston's big population boom continues with this many new residents each day.* CultureMap Houston. https://houston.culturemap.com/news/city-life/04-23-19-houston-the-woodlands-sugar-land-population-growth-us-census/

Goodyear, S. (2014, April 2). A Ranking of the Most Sprawling U.S. Metro Areas, and Why You Should Care. Bloomberg.Com. https://www.bloomberg.com/news/articles/2014-04-02/a-ranking-of-the-most-sprawling-u-s-metro-areas-and-why-you-should-care

National Weather Service. (2014). *United States Flood Loss Report -Water Year 2014.* https://www.weather.gov/media/water/WY14%20Flood%20Loss%20Summary.pdf

Neal, Z. P., & Watling Neal, J. (2012). The Public School as a Public Good: Direct and Indirect Pathways to Community Satisfaction. *Journal of Urban Affairs, 34*(5), 469–486.

Romero, D. (2015, February 18). *L.A. Is America's "Least Sprawling" City!?* LA Weekly. https://www.laweekly.com/l-a-is-americas-least-sprawling-city/

ScienceDaily. (2018). *Houston's urban sprawl increased rainfall, flooding during Hurricane Harvey.* https://www.sciencedaily.com/releases/2018/11/181114131957.htm

Stolark, J. (2014). *USGS Finds Growing Urban Sprawl in Southeast Rivals Threat of Climate Change.* https://www.eesi.org/articles/view/usgs-finds-growing-urban-sprawl-in-southeast-rivals-threat-of-climate-chang

Tiebout, C. M. (1956). A Pure Theory of Local Expenditures. *Journal of Political Economy, 64*(5), 416–424. https://doi.org/10.1086/257839

United States Census Bureau. (2010). *QuickFacts-Los Angeles County.* https://www.census.gov/quickfacts/fact/table/losangelescountycalifornia

CONCLUSION

The past few years have been flush with topics that could have been included in this book, but 2020 in particular has been a banner year for challenges to federalism. It might even be possible to do a version of this text using only stories, case studies, and research about the Coronavirus alone. The choice between the responsibility (or not) of the federal government to step in with emergency assistance versus the expectation (or not) that states be able to fend for themselves has been a struggle fraught with tension. What is the responsibility of the federal government to send money and equipment to states when something like a pandemic happens? Is it necessary to send help to all states equally? And if not, on what basis is a president allowed to make these choices? Because there is nothing in the Constitution that says that the president can't send more ventilators to states that he likes better. At least not unless it is for reasons that break civil rights laws.

But while the news cycle has been eaten up by the virus, the election, and the cancellation of "Keeping up with the Kardashians," there have been seemingly a million other major events taking place. Iowa became the last state to grant voting rights to former felons. College athletes in some states will be able to get paid for their appearances in things like ads and video games. Natural disasters—millions of acres of forest fires, so many hurricanes that we ran out of names for them, and a wind event called a derecho that almost no one had even heard of—have devastated areas of the country, and because of all of the other distractions, many people aren't even aware of the ones that didn't occur in their own region. 21 states have proposed legislation to legalize sports betting within their borders. The minimum wage went up in 24 states and 48 cities and counties in 2020. Harvey Weinstein went to prison.

We focus so much on national politics. It's sexy and dramatic. It is particularly tawdry right now, with all of the divisiveness and vitriol; it would be difficult to get more of a spectacle by staying home from school and watching old reruns of Jerry Springer. But remember what you learned earlier in this book: although the U.S. Congress is the most professionalized legislative body in the United States, it is not the most productive. All of those action items listed in the last paragraph? They happened at the state and local levels.

And even with the response to the Covid-19 Pandemic, we saw significant action on the parts of state and local governments. You read earlier about how in emergencies the federal government generally steps in because of their money and access to equipment and expertise … but this particular emergency has been different from other emergencies in many ways. So, when Washington didn't issue nation-wide emergency orders like many other countries did, states started to act. March saw Ohio issue a quarantine order and Arizona secure a fund to pay for housing, small business loans, and food bank needs. In June, Illinois halted evictions and New York began allowing people to appear in court via video link. Even though most state governments don't have the kind of money needed to really shore up their economies during a pandemic, they did what they do, which is use the powers granted to them in the U.S. Constitution and got to work doing what they were able.

INDEX

Allen v. City of Long Beach 43
amendment 22–23, 28–31, 66, 68, 99,
    100; Fourteenth Amendment 99–100
American Legislative Exchange Council
    (ALEC) 34–36, 62, 69–73
Attorney General 87–89, 106, 117
audit 116, 118

Bentley, Robert 86–88
Black, Sandra 138
block grants 16, 18–19
Bloomberg, Michael 1, 66
Boards of Elections 54, 56
Brown, Jerry 92–95
Brownback, Sam 5, 14, 118
Buckley v. Valeo 57, 69
budget 17, 23, 26, 38–50, 85, 90–91, 108,
    112, 120, 123
Bureau of Land Management 20, 22
bureaucracy 108–119

California Rule 44–45
campaign 57–58, 61, 65, 91, 114; finance
    36, 62, 66–69, 71, 80, 86–87, 90, 124
capitalism 41
Carter, Jimmy 9
Castle Doctrine 70
categorical grants 16, 18–19
census 9, 14, 32, 37, 67, 69, 93, 96, 103,
    111, 132, 134, 139
Chambers, Ernie 30, 37

Christie, Chris 18, 45
citizen legislature 78
Citizens United v. FEC 35–36, 62, 66, 69
city manager 123, 125–126
Civil Rights Act 1964 9, 18, 23, 62, 65, 74
civil service 91, 112
climate 1, 92–96, 134–135
Clinton, Bill 9
comparative method 3–14
competition 66, 113, 134, 138
compliance 35, 62, 83
compulsory voting 52, 54
concurrent powers 17, 19
conflict of interest 80–81
Constitution: federal 19, 20, 22–23, 56,
    63, 66, 72, 86, 99, 106, 140, 141;
    state 27–37, 68–69, 90, 97
contract rights 43–45
council-manager system 123–126, 129
cyber security 54, 56, 60

decentralization 55–56
Democrat 47, 91; Democratic party 8–11,
    61–65
Department of Education Office of Civil
    Rights 15, 24–25
depopulation 129
Desert Lands Entry Act 1877 20
development 21, 132–135
devolution 10
Dillon's Rule 31, 34, 37, 120

disenfranchisement 57, 60
due process 98–100, 111, 118

economy 3, 5, 8, 13, 39–41, 46, 72,
   93–94, 126
Elazar, Daniel 4–5, 10
emergency declaration 11, 17, 122–123,
   141
environment 1, 16, 29, 72, 85, 91–96
executive order 45, 48
exurbs 131, 135

Federal Land Policy and Management
   Act 1976 20, 22
Federal Sex Offender Registry 83
federalism 15–26, 70, 72, 81, 83, 94–95,
   122–123
Federal Emergency Management
   Agency (FEMA) 17, 19
fiscal year 45–48
flood(ing) 15–18, 130, 133–136, 139
fuel standards 94–95
furlough 46, 48–49

Gaebler, Ted 112–113
Gerber, Alan 52–54
Good Neighbor Policy 21–22
Gott, J.S. 97–98
government shutdown 45–50
Great Recession 47–48, 127, 129
Green, Donald 52–54
greenhouse gas emissions 1, 93–95
Greitens, Eric 86–88

Hawthorne effect 53, 60
Holmes, Justin 57–59
home rule 31–35, 37
Homestead Act 1862 20–21
Honest Elections 68–69
hurricane 16–18, 122, 133–134, 140
hybrid legislature 79, 81

immigration 23, 126–129
impeachment 86–89, 96, 102
impermeable surfaces 133, 135
in loco parentis 97–100, 107
incumbency 85, 89–92
inflation 39, 41

jobs 5, 8, 40, 41, 43, 44, 72, 78, 81, 85,
   90, 94, 108–113, 118, 123, 125
judicial selection 103

laboratories of democracy 6, 11–12
Larimer, Christopher 52–54
legacy costs 42–43, 45
legislative capacity 79, 81, 83
legislative professionalism 79, 81
liability 44, 107, 116, 118
Liadley, Thomas 131–132
Lipsky, Michael 113–114, 118
Liquor Control Commission 104–106

mandatory minimum 101, 103
Mayor-council system 123, 125–126
McNeal, Ramona 57–59
median income 103, 106
Merton, Robert K. 113, 119
metropolitan area 127, 130, 133
mobility 138
model legislation/bills 30, 62, 69–73
motivation: extrinsic 52, 54;
   intrinsic 52, 54

Nation's Report Card 23, 25
national debt 42, 44, 50
National Rifle Association (NRA) 30,
   37, 70
Neal, Zachary 137–138
New Public Management 112, 115

Osborne, David 112–113, 119

pension 38, 42, 43–45
Persky, Aaron 101–102, 106
petition 59, 66, 80, 101, 113
Political Action Committee (PAC) 68,
   124, 126
political culture 4–6, 10, 27, 65
political participation 57–59
population density 12, 83, 93, 132, 133
preemption 27, 34–37
Public Employee Retirement System
   (PERS) 44

Reagan, Ronald 21, 64, 114–115
recall election 91–92, 101–103
recession 39, 41, 46–48, 127, 129
regulations 21, 32, 35, 66, 72, 82,
   91, 94, 98, 108, 112, 115–118,
   123, 134
Reinventing Government 112
representation: descriptive 75–78;
   substantive 78
Republican 9, 16, 18, 35–36, 46–47, 94

Republican party 9, 47, 61–65, 91, 114, 118
reservation 103–107
resignation 86–89
Roberts, Matty 120–122
Roosevelt, Franklin Delano 8, 63

Sagebrush Rebellion 21
schools 6, 15, 22–25, 32, 36, 39–40, 72, 82, 98–100, 102, 107, 110, 111, 114, 127, 130, 135–139, 141
Schwab, Caleb 115–118
self-government/self-governance 32, 34, 37
slacktivism 59–60
social media 58–60, 121
social pressure 51–53
sociodemographics 6, 10, 129
sprawl 4, 130–135, 139
Stand Your Ground 70, 74
State Auditor 87, 89
State Ethics Commission 87, 102
state sovereignty 19, 22, 31, 34, 37
storm surge 17, 133, 125
street-level bureaucrat 113, 115, 118
suburbs 91, 131, 133
Supremacy Clause 22, 25

Tausanovitch, Chris 125
term limits 90, 92, 96, 124
Tiebout, Charles 135–138
Title IX 23
Title VI 23
traffic 93, 124, 131–133, 139
trained incapacity 113, 115
trifectas 35, 47
Truman, Harry 9, 63
Turner, Brock 101–102

undocumented workers 126, 128
unfunded liabilities 42, 44
unions 44, 91, 111, 118
university 38–41, 97–101, 106, 109

variance 3, 6, 10, 12, 25, 83
Veblen, Thorstein 113, 119
Von Mises, Ludwick 112, 119
voter turnout 4, 29, 51–52, 54, 60, 120

Walker, Scott 89–92, 96
Wallace, George 9, 64
Warshaw, Christopher 125
Watling Neal, Jennifer 137–138
Weber, Max 112–115

For Product Safety Concerns and Information please contact our EU
representative GPSR@taylorandfrancis.com
Taylor & Francis Verlag GmbH, Kaufingerstraße 24, 80331 München, Germany

9 780367 174552